THE WRITING BOOK

THE WRITING BOOK

JOAN G. ROLOFF

Chaffey College

ROBERT C. WYLDER

California State University
Long Beach

GLENCOE PUBLISHING CO., INC.
Encino, California

Copyright © 1978 by Glencoe Publishing Co., Inc.

Printed in the United States of America

Glencoe Publishing Co., Inc.
17337 Ventura Boulevard
Encino, California 91316

Collier Macmillan Canada, Ltd.

Library of Congress Catalog Card Number: 77-79241

2 3 4 5 6 7 8 9   80 79 78

ISBN 0-02-477120-1

CONTENTS

SECTION 1 READINGS FOR WRITING PRACTICE

SECTION 2 WRITING GUIDE

SECTION **3** **PICTURES FOR WRITING PRACTICE**

SECTION **4** **HANDBOOK**

PREFACE

The Writing Book is designed to help students learn to write English prose effectively. Although any student at any level of proficiency in the skill of writing should find this book useful, it is particularly appropriate for those who have not yet achieved the competence needed for success in school and in the world of work. It assumes that anyone who speaks and reads English can learn to write it if provided with adequate instruction, adequate opportunity to practice writing, and enough time to consolidate the skills acquired.

The book provides the first two, instruction and practice. The time to be devoted to learning the skills of writing will depend upon the student, the course, and other factors over which the book has no control. It does allow for whatever pace the student and teacher decide upon; some students will be able to acquire writing competence faster than others. Completion of all of the assignments and exercises may not be necessary or even possible within the time frame of a given term. The object is to achieve skill in writing, at whatever pace and by whatever means are appropriate.

The Writing Book consists of four parts. Each is preceded by an introduction explaining what it is and how to use it. The first section contains twenty brief reading selections, each followed by writing exercises. It offers practice in close reading as well as in composing, and the writing exercises are progressive in difficulty throughout the section. The second section contains instruction in the writing process, a sample paper, and two writing exercises which stress the overall composition of a piece of writing. The third section consists of photographs with accompanying writing exercises. It deals with traditional rhetorical principles and requires the student to use progressively more abstract thought and judgment. The last section is a selective handbook of grammar, punctuation, usage, and spelling, with exercises which include both writing and editing.

A brief word about this selective handbook is in order here. Of the myriad principles and "rules" which govern the composition of Standard Written English, we have concentrated on those most often misunderstood or misapplied by students who have trouble with the conventions of that medium. Our choices are not random; they are based on a careful tabulation of the types of errors most frequently found in over three thousand student themes in three different parts of the country. In addition, approximately half of the sentences in the "Sentence Practice" section that accompanies each rule are actual student sentences—containing actual student errors—taken from the more than three thousand themes. We believe that if students master the forty principles or rules in this handbook, their written compositions will be relatively free of common errors of convention.

No book can by itself teach a student to write. No teacher alone can do it. Both can help the student to learn, however, if the student wants to do so. The student alone must do the learning.

Available for use with this text is *Tests to Accompany The Writing Book*. This booklet contains three tests. Each has forty sections, keyed to the forty entries in the Handbook portion of *The Writing Book*. The three tests are parallel and can therefore be used to assess progress towards the mastery of the conventions involved in the composition of Standard Written English. Our suggestion is that students use the first test as a diagnostic test, in order to ascertain their specific areas of weakness in those conventions. The two other tests can then be used in one of two ways: in a one-term course, Test 2 can be a midterm check-up, Test 3 a final examination. In a two-term course, Tests 2 and 3 can be used as finals for the two terms. A test record sheet is provided with these three tests, so that students can record their progressive scores in each of the forty sections.

Also available is a comprehensive Teacher's Guide, which provides answers to tests 2 and 3 of the test booklet. Additionally, it contains information on the audience for and features of *The Writing Book*, as well as suggestions for presenting and augmenting the material in the text.

We wish to thank Virginia Brosseit for her work in writing or adapting the reading selections in Part 1.

THE WRITING BOOK

READINGS FOR WRITING PRACTICE

INTRODUCTION

In this section are twenty selections, each followed by instructions for writing activities. You should read each assigned selection carefully. Probably your instructor will arrange for some class discussion of the selections in order to answer any questions that may arise and to allow for exchange of ideas that grow out of the reading. If there is no class time available for such discussion, you may want to arrange it with one or more of your classmates outside of class; interaction is very important in complete understanding.

The writing activities following the readings range in difficulty from easy to hard. You should be able to do the earlier ones with little or no trouble. It is important that you follow the instructions provided and that you write whatever is asked for, since you can learn to write only by writing practice.

Practice alone, of course, is not enough: the feedback you get from your instructor and your classmates will let you know whether you have written effectively or not. Even though you may be hesitant to write something because you are not confident that you can do it well, try your best and depend upon your instructor and other students for help. That's the only way to learn how to write effectively. It's something like learning to ride a bicycle; you didn't do that without some help, but you kept on practicing until you could do it alone. Writing is more complicated than riding a bicycle, but the process of learning to do it is much the same.

For some of the exercises, space for your writing has been provided within the book itself. For other exercises, you will be asked to write on separate paper. If you double space and write on only one side of the paper, you will make it easier for someone to comment on what you have written.

Now, on to reading and to writing practice.

THOSE GOLDEN ARCHES

There can't be many people in the United States who haven't heard of McDonald's and its golden arches. Nor can there be many who have not partaken of McDonald's famous hamburgers, fries, and shakes. It may soon be possible to state that there are few people in the *world* who have not heard of the golden arches. There are now McDonald's restaurants in Japan, The Netherlands, Germany, Australia, Puerto Rico, the Virgin Islands, Costa Rica, Guam, and Canada.

The McDonald brothers started their now-famous hamburger business in California. At that time their operation was something new: fifteen-cent hamburgers, with self-service. They concentrated on making their business unique by streamlining food preparation and by insisting on quality foods. In a short time they were opening other units in the Southwest.

Then, in 1954, a man named Ray Kroc came along. Realizing the uniqueness of the McDonald's restaurants, Kroc made a deal with the McDonald brothers whereby he could franchise the operation for a percentage of the profits. Kroc himself opened the first franchised McDonald's in April, 1955, in Des Plaines, Illinois.

By the time the number of McDonald's restaurants in the country had grown to over 200, Mr. Kroc had bought the formulas, trademark, and name from the McDonald brothers. In the years since that time, the growth of the corporation has continued by leaps and bounds. There are now several thousand McDonald's restaurants in operation all over the United States.

Anyone who wants a license to open his or her own franchised McDonald's restaurant must be prepared, both money-wise and personality-wise. McDonald's officials say they immediately reject any applicant who doesn't seem to like people, since the big emphasis in the McDonald's operation is on pleasing people with good food, good service, and attractive surroundings.

After an applicant for a license has been accepted, he or she must go to school. The school, called Hamburger University and located in Elk Grove Village, Illinois, is operated by the McDonald Corporation for the training and education of new managers. The nine-day course is hard and concentrated. The instructors use a variety of educational aids, such as overhead projectors and closed-circuit TV, in teaching their classes. Subjects studied in the course include food preparation, store and appliance maintenance, purchasing, accounting, and report writing.

McDonald's officials aim at keeping their stores consistent and uniform in matters of food, dress, and decor. Customers like and expect this consistency, officials say; and children, in particular, depend on it.

With children on their side, how can McDonald's restaurants lose? Is there a kid alive, no matter whether he can read signs or not, who doesn't know when his parents are approaching a McDonald's? A kid can spot those golden arches anywhere!

JUAN GOES TO HEAVEN

A MEXICAN FOLKTALE RETOLD

Back in the time of Juan Garcia, there was a great flood in Northern Mexico. And when the flood was at its height, washing the helpless people and pigs of Monterrey into the arroyo, Juan Garcia and his gray horse swam to the rescue. Through their heroic efforts that night, twelve women, six pigs, and four men were saved from drowning.

Throughout his long life the fame of the mighty Juan Garcia spread across the land. He soon became the greatest hero Mexico had ever known, credited with rescuing fifteen—or was it twenty or twenty-five?—people from the Monterrey flood.

At last Juan Garcia died. Saint Peter's assistant answered Juan's knock on the door of Heaven. When Juan explained who he was—namely, the hero of the Monterrey flood—the assistant looked puzzled. "I'm sorry, but I never heard of you," he said.

"And *I* never heard of *you*," was Juan's curt response. "Send for Saint Peter himself."

The assistant called Saint Peter and explained the situation. "And he says he's a hero," finished the assistant, doubt plain in his voice.

"That's just what I am!" exclaimed Juan Garcia. "I saved twenty people from the Monterrey flood and am certainly entitled to a place in Heaven."

After examining the records, Saint Peter let Juan Garcia inside and said he'd introduce him to some of the residents. But Juan said he preferred to introduce himself.

Going up to Napoleon he said, "I am Juan Garcia, hero of the Monterrey flood. I saved the lives of twenty-five people!"

Napoleon welcomed Juan to Heaven. Then Juan went over to Julius Caesar, saying, "I am Juan Garcia, hero of Monterrey. I dashed into the terrible flood and rescued thirty people!"

Julius Caesar gave Juan a warm welcome, as did Henry VIII, George Washington, and many others, even Pancho Villa. But there was one old man, all wrapped up in a sarape, who said not a word to Juan Garcia.

No matter how carefully and no matter how loudly Juan explained his great heroism, the old man did not respond. Even when Juan shouted, "Don't you understand? I saved thirty-five people from the Monterrey flood!" the old man sat unmoved.

Then Juan complained to Saint Peter that the old man was making fun of him by not acknowledging his presence. Saint Peter went over to the old man and said, "This is Juan Garcia, hero of the Monterrey flood."

The old man lifted his sarape, looked Juan Garcia in the eye, and said, "Pfffft!"

"What does he mean by that?" gasped Juan.

"This man's name is Noah," said Saint Peter, "and he doesn't give a hoot about your Monterrey flood."

"GOING-OUTSIDE" CLASS FOR ESKIMO STUDENTS

"Our Eskimo students must be taught how to survive in the Arctic," says the principal of the expensive new high school in Frobisher Bay, Northwest Territories, Canada.

Believe it or not, he isn't kidding. He goes on to tell the interviewer that most Eskimo children in this era have never lived in an igloo nor ridden in a dog sled nor hunted for seal nor fished through the ice. So they must go to the white man's school in order to learn how.

How has this sorry state of affairs arisen? Again, it's through the white man. In his zeal for exploitation of the animal and mineral riches of the tundra, the white man has also exploited the Eskimo. Wherever he has gone, the white man has taken along his weapons, his dubious moral values, and his booze. White missionaries and teachers have further muddled the situation by taking away the Eskimo religion and culture and substituting brands which many Eskimos can't or won't buy.

Some Eskimos have succeeded in the white man's world, but they are relatively few in number. The number who have kept their own culture, yet adapted to Western ways, is perhaps a little larger. But by far the largest number of Eskimos live in a no-man's land of despair, idleness, and futility, their misery merely dulled by alcohol. With their own culture frowned upon by the white man and his brand of education forced down their throats, what are the Eskimos to do? There is no industry for them to turn to, and nothing but the most unrewarding, boring jobs are offered them as a means of livelihood.

Now that one generation has lost almost all instinct and will for survival, education experts are planning how to re-instill them into young people. The new high school has instituted a hunting and fishing course and a class in how to make harpoons. A few students at a time will participate in the going-outside class where they will learn how to live out in the cold. They will be taught how to make igloos and sleep in them—sure to be a shock to kids who've always lived in houses!

Also on the curriculum will be a course in Eskimo soapstone carving, an art long prized by collectors and museums. What the students will think of the ancient art compared to their courses in electronics and mechanics and home economics is anybody's guess, particularly since the equipment they work with (engines, electric stoves and dishwashers, and automatic washers and dryers) is nonexistent in their native villages.

The biggest gripe that white men have against the Eskimos is that they won't stay with a job once they find one. An Eskimo says it goes against his cultural freedom to be chained to an 8:00 A.M. to 5:00 P.M. job. Another reason for their walking out on the job must certainly be the government handouts that rob the Eskimos of motivation to help themselves. If the new high school curriculum, including the going-outside class, can help young Eskimos find their way in a world whose complexities boggle the minds of many white people, it will be well worthwhile.

Writing Practice

Following is a list of words or phrases from the story you have just read. For each word or phrase, write a sentence of at least ten words to tell about some information contained in the story. Example: booze. The booze introduced into the life of the Eskimos has had a bad effect on them.

1. survive _The Eskimos' ability to survive in the arctic shows their adaptability in cold climate._

2. Arctic _The arctic region gets so cold in winter that the temperature drops to minus 60° below zero._

3. igloo _If you are not well adapted to cold weather you will never like to live in an igloo._

4. Eskimo _An Eskimo will never accept a job that will keep him or her indoors for eight continuous hours._

5. going-outside class _Going-outside class seems to be a favorite of the athletic type of students._

Write two or three sentences about the skills needed for survival in modern city life.

In order to be able to survive in a city, a person must learn modern trades, like electronics, computer science, modern business technology, and the ability to learn how to operate electrical appliances.

15

THATCHED-ROOFERY IS NOT A SPOOFERY

As recently as ten years ago the picturesque thatched-roof cottages dotting the English countryside were scorned by the landowning gentry. Shabby and small and usually without plumbing, the unwanted cottages were leveled or burned. Now there is a sudden boom in thatched roofs. Cottages sporting roofs of thatched straw or reed sell for prices almost twenty times higher than they did a decade ago.

The boom has been credited by some to the London weekend crowd. They want beauty and charm and don't seem to mind a little impracticability thrown in. (Undoubtedly impracticability is easier to take when you don't *have* to live with it.) Even the British government is getting into the act by official preservation of the best examples of thatched-roof cottages.

Like everything else, a thatched roof has its pros and cons. On the pro side is the thickness of the roof, usually about a foot. It keeps noise out, and it insulates against the weather. But watch out once the roof begins to deteriorate! Birds find it a cozy home, and their incessant chirping can drive you to find your own cozy home elsewhere. Mice, too, are attracted to a thatched roof that has begun to fall apart. While the presence of our little furred and feathered friends may be no more than irritating, there's a very real danger connected with these roofs. They can very quickly explode into flames.

It's hard to tell whether roof thatchers themselves are happy about the boom. The trade was on the verge of dying out, with perhaps only about four hundred master thatchers left in England. Now that there's more work than the old guard can handle, young men have begun flocking to thatchery, to learn the intricacies of the craft. But thatchers have long been noted for their independence; they've led lonely lives and seem to prefer it that way. If they choose not to take on a job, they don't hesitate to say so.

Thatching is hard work. About four or five tons of reed or straw are required for a two or three-bedroom cottage. It takes one thatcher (most of them prefer to work alone) perhaps four or five weeks to complete the job, in weather that is often cold and windy.

Because of the great demand for thatched roofs, an English company has come out with a fiberglass thatch. It's guaranteed bird and mouse proof and can be put up in less than a week. Are conventional thatchers worried about this threat to their jobs? Not by a long shot. They say that man can't improve on nature. So, not to be compared to Browning's "Home-Thoughts, from Abroad," here's a tribute to roof thatchers—

> With Mother Nature at the helm,
> Long live thatched-roofery in England's realm!

Writing Practice

Following is a list of words or phrases from the report you have just read. For each word or phrase, write a sentence of at least ten words to convey information contained in the report. Example: insulates. A thatched roof insulates a house against winter cold and summer heat.

1. boom _____
    _____
    _____

2. chirping _____
    _____
    _____

3. thatchers _____
    _____
    _____

4. thatched-roof cottager _____
    _____
    _____

5. explode _____
    _____
    _____

Write three or four sentences about the sorts of roofs found in your neighborhood, comparing them to thatched roofs in terms of both looks and practicality.

_____
_____
_____

_____

_____

_____

_____

_____

_____

_____

THE LOST BIRD

A LATIN AMERICAN FOLKTALE RETOLD

One day long ago the eagle who was king over all the birds called them to a meeting. When the birds had assembled, the eagle noticed that one of them was completely naked. Not a single feather did this bird have to call his own.

The king was highly offended. "This will never do! Throw that bird out," he ordered.

The dove, a tender-hearted creature, said timidly, "If each of us would give him a feather, he would be properly dressed. I'll be happy to give the first one."

The peacock and some of the other birds were against the idea; the prospect of a rival with a many-colored coat aroused jealousy in their feathered breasts. However, King Eagle agreed to the proposal if someone could be found to act as sponsor.

The owl, feared and respected by all the birds, said sleepily, "I will be his sponsor."

At once the birds began to give feathers to the naked one. From the cardinal, the robin, and the scarlet tanager he received red feathers; the bluebird and the bluejay provided blue feathers; the parrot and the hummingbird green. The canary gave a yellow feather; the oriole gave orange; from the wren came brown; and from the quail a speckled feather.

It wasn't long until the naked one had feathers in plenty, and their colors surpassed even those of the rainbow. He was, without question, the most beautiful bird who ever lived. But he became exceedingly proud and boastful. Indeed, his pride was so great that he refused even to speak to the other birds.

The next day King Eagle called all the birds to another meeting. As they sat in front of him, he noticed that the bird who had been naked was not among them. "This will never do!" he screamed. "That bird must be brought back." Turning to the owl, King Eagle ordered him, as the sponsor, to bring in the runaway.

The owl made excuses: the sun was too bright; he was sleepy; he was too blind to hunt in the daytime; he would look for the truant when evening fell.

King Eagle would have had the owl taken prisoner, but again the kind-hearted dove intervened. "I will search for the lost bird," she offered, and she set out immediately. The other members of the dove family went with her, and all through the woods could be heard their calls of "Coo, coo, coo." Even the roadrunner, who could only say, "Croo, croo, croo," helped in the search.

The lost bird was never found. But the doves still call softly for him morning and night, and the roadrunner spends his days running up one trail and down another, stopping now and then to look in all directions. Even the owl searches faithfully, calling "Who, who, who," in the dusk of evening.

Writing Practice

Answer each of the following questions with one or two words. Then expand your answers into a complete sentence. Example: Who was the king of the birds? The eagle. The eagle was the king over all the birds.

1. What did the dove propose that each of the birds should give to the naked bird?

    _____

    _____

    _____

    _____

2. Who agreed to be the sponsor of the naked bird? _____

    _____

    _____

3. What did the naked bird become after he had received colorful feathers from the

    other birds? _____

    _____

    _____

    _____

4. Did the dove ever find the boastful colorful bird? _____

    _____

    _____

    _____

5. What does the owl say in his search for the bird in the dusk of evening?

    _____

    _____

_____

_____

Write four or five related sentences about your favorite animal.

_____

_____

_____

_____

_____

_____

_____

_____

_____

_____

_____

WHAT DOES A PRAYING MANTIS PRAY FOR?

The praying mantis is a weird-looking insect, little changed from mantis fossils which date back 40 million years. The dinosaurs and the saber-toothed tigers and the mastodons couldn't make it in a changing environment; but the mantis kept right on devouring everything in sight, and today it is the gardener's best friend.

The mantis is not a fussy eater. It enjoys cockroaches, grasshoppers, flies, wasps, caterpillars, moths, beetles, and even an occasional honeybee. When it's on the hunt, any insect in its path is not long for this world. The mantis raises its forelegs not to pray, but to get into striking position. It remains motionless in this position for its unlucky victim to come within reach as long as is necessary. Then WHAM!—the forelegs stretch out, grab the prey, and haul it up to be eaten. That tidbit down the hatch, the mantis washes its face, cat-fashion, first with one foreleg, then the other. By the time the cleanliness routine has been completed, another victim has wandered into the vicinity.

If ordinary mantis meals sound like savage affairs, consider the sex life of the praying mantis. Courtship alone is hazardous for the male; the wedding is purely disaster. No matter how cautiously he approaches his intended bride, the male is likely to get embraced and eaten by her before achieving his goal. If he can sneak up behind her, he may be able to mate with her. About one in four male mantises does manage the feat and gets away with his life. The other three get lassoed by the female's foreleg, hauled off her back, and gobbled up.

The female doesn't get away with it for long, however. After mating, she hangs upside down on a twig or stem and spins out her egg case. When she has completed this important function, she dies. Come spring, the egg case produces as many as 300 baby mantises. After a few hours of drying in the sun, the whole cycle starts over again by them. But they do more good than people realize: with mantises around to destroy insect pests, we can avoid the use of dangerous pesticides.

So what does a praying mantis actually pray for? Not much, really. Just a good square meal, a long, nonstop meal.

Writing Practice

Answer each of the following questions in as few words as possible. Then expand your answer into a complete sentence. (If your answer is already a complete sentence, rewrite it in another way.) Example: Why does the mantis raise his forelegs? To get into a striking position. The mantis raises his forelegs in order to get into a striking position.

1. Why is the praying mantis considered the gardener's best friend? _____

   _____

   _____

   _____

2. What may happen to the male mantis when trying to mate with the female?

   _____

   _____

   _____

   _____

3. What does the mantis eat? _____

   _____

   _____

   _____

4. How many mantises mate with females and get away alive? _____

   _____

   _____

   _____

5. The female mantis dies after performing what important function? _____

   _____

   _____

_____

_____

Write several related sentences about other useful insects or about insect pests or nuisances and the harm they do.

_____

_____

_____

_____

_____

_____

_____

_____

_____

_____

THE ORIGIN OF THE MOSQUITO

A VIETNAMESE LEGEND RETOLD

There was once a farmer in Vietnam who married a beautiful young woman. It so happened that this young couple was poor, and the farmer had to work very hard in his rice paddy to make a living. Even so, with their youth and good health, they could have managed a comfortable life it it hadn't been for one thing—the wife was lazy, yet she wanted all kinds of luxuries.

The husband was so much in love with his wife that he never noticed this flaw in her character. She died suddenly, and he almost went crazy with grief; he even refused to let her be buried. Instead, he sold everything he owned, bought a boat, and sailed away with her coffin.

Eventually he came to an amazing island where all kinds of rare fruits and flowers grew. The only person on the island was a man who, at first glance, appeared to be old because he was white-haired and used a cane for walking. Then the husband noticed the man's young, sparkling eyes, and he realized that this was the spirit of medicine. The husband fell at the spirit's feet, begging him to bring his young wife back to life.

Knowing of her bad qualities, the spirit hesitated to do this. "Young man," he said kindly, "she's not worth it. I'm afraid you'll regret it if I let her come back to you."

But the husband begged so hard that the spirit finally agreed. He told the young man to cut his finger and let three drops of blood fall on his wife's body.

Sure enough, she returned to life. Both husband and wife were overjoyed. They thanked the spirit of medicine and went on their way.

But now see how that young woman repaid her husband's devotion!

When their boat was moored in a harbor so the husband could go ashore and buy food, a big boat came alongside. The rich owner of the big boat was quite taken with the young wife and she with him. So off they sailed together, leaving the poor young husband frantic with grief again.

He pursued the lovers for a whole month before he caught up with them. But no matter how the husband begged and pleaded, his wife refused to come back to him.

Finally he saw that she was no good. "I want no part of you," he told her, "and I don't want you to have any part of me. Give me back those three drops of blood I gave you."

"Who wants them?" she said scornfully, and proceeded to cut her finger. The minute the first drop of blood oozed out, she fell down dead.

But she was too stubborn to leave this world altogether. She got herself turned into a small insect and began pestering her husband unmercifully. Day after day she zoomed around him, trying to stab him for the three drops of blood that would turn her into a human again.

And that, as not so many people know, is how the mosquito came into being.

Writing Practice

Following are five starter sentences. After each, write another sentence, of at least ten words, related to it and drawn from the legend you have just read. Example: Once a farmer in Vietnam married a beautiful young woman who had one flaw. She was lazy but still wanted luxuries of all kinds.

1. The beautiful wife died suddenly. _____

    _____

    _____

    _____

2. The old man said, "I don't think you should try to bring her back from the dead."

    _____

    _____

    _____

    _____

3. The young husband cut his finger and dripped three drops of blood on his wife's

    corpse. _____

    _____

    _____

    _____

4. The husband moored and went ashore to buy food. _____

    _____

    _____

    _____

5. The wife was transformed into a mosquito. _____

    _____

_____

_____

Write several related sentences about one or more problems people often have in
relationships with other people.

_____

_____

_____

_____

_____

_____

_____

_____

_____

_____

SILENCE - IS IT REALLY GOLDEN?

Visitors to the city: does every honking horn, grinding gear, and the endless rush of traffic grate on your nerves? And you who visit the country: do you detest the loud-mouthed birds and animals who disturb your rest?

City dwellers themselves often complain of the noise they're subjected to. Some city governments have even passed ordinances regulating automobile horn blowing, and industrial planners constantly seek ways of lowering decibel levels.

Country dwellers don't escape great volumes of sound, either. Farm machinery and trucks are ponderous, with noise that matches their size. Many factories, seeking cheap land and labor, have moved to small communities, bringing their noise with them.

Scientists tell us that noise is bad for us. Noise at certain levels causes loss of hearing in human beings. At higher levels it can even cause actual pain. If you don't believe the scientists, try tooting a flute or clarinet for your pet dog!

What are we to do to preserve ourselves from the destructive effects of noise? Should we lock ourselves into sound-proofed, windowless cells?

Better not, say scientists, unless your cell is well padded and you are under restraints; for they have discovered that both human beings and animals are unable to tolerate utter silence and complete darkness without cracking up.

"Imagine," says one scientist, "that you're in a situation where you can hear every heartbeat clearly and every breath sounds like a strong wind blowing."

Perhaps we should be grateful for the horns and gears and factory whistles, the tractors and trucks and roosters that crow at dawn. It seems that such noises are easier for us to adapt to than noisy breathing and a loud beating heart.

Writing Practice

Following are five starter sentences. After each, write two sentences, of at least ten words each, related to the starter sentence and drawn from the preceding report. Example: The residents of the country and small towns are bothered by noise. Farm machinery is noisy, and many factories have moved to small towns. It seems that wherever we may live, noise has become a part of our daily lives.

1. It has been demonstrated that noise is bad for us. _____

_____

_____

_____

_____

_____

2. Some city dwellers have complained about the noise they are subjected to.

_____

_____

_____

_____

_____

_____

3. Maybe we should be glad that gears clatter and whistles blow. _____

_____

_____

_____

_____

_____

4. We should not seek to keep out noise entirely. _____

_____

_____

_____

_____

5. Noise at high levels can cause actual pain. _____

_____

_____

_____

Write several related sentences about ways in which noise is useful to us in modern society.

_____

_____

_____

_____

_____

_____

_____

_____

_____

_____

_____

THE BEST SELLER YOU CAN'T BUY

As everybody knows, the Bible is often called the world's best-selling book. But there is a Bible you can't buy at any bookstore, and that's the Gideon Bible.

While you cannot purchase a Gideon Bible, you're welcome to read one any time you stay in a hotel, motel, or jail. Many leading hotel chains insist that a Gideon Bible be present in a room before guests are assigned. Others go a step further by making sure that every room has a Bible opened on top of the night table. Accommodations may not be so plush in the local lockup, but you can be reasonably sure of finding a Gideon Bible.

Distribution of the Bibles is taken care of by a group of laymen known as Gideons, International. There are over twenty thousand of these Christian businessmen in the United States and eighty-eight foreign countries.

The Gideon Society was organized in July, 1899, when three traveling men met in a Wisconsin hotel. They realized that many Christian salesmen traveled around the country, spending lonely evenings in hotel rooms. Their answer to this problem was to place Bibles in hotel rooms for salesmen to read. The cost of the Bibles is taken care of by free-will offerings.

The name of the Gideon Society comes from the Bible: Judges, Chapter 7. Gideon, an important figure in Jewish history, delivered Israel from the Midianite tribe.

"More and more people," says one Gideon, "are looking to the Bible for the answers to their problems." Perhaps that is why Gideon Society members find that they are making more replacements than ever before in hotels, motels, and hospitals. Apparently there are people who believe in simply helping themselves to what cannot be bought.

Writing Practice

Following are five starter sentences. After each write three related sentences of at least ten words each. You may draw the information for your sentences from the preceding anecdote or from your own knowledge.

1. Gideon Bibles cannot be bought at a bookstore. _____

    _____

    _____

    _____

    _____

2. The Bible is the world's best-selling book. _____

    _____

    _____

    _____

    _____

    _____

3. The Gideon Society has been distributing free Bibles for over three quarters of a

    century. _____

    _____

    _____

    _____

    _____

4. Recently the rate of replacement of Gideon Bibles has increased. _____

    _____

_____

_____

_____

_____

5.   One Gideon asserts that nowadays more and more people are depending upon

the Bible for solutions to their problems. _____

_____

_____

_____

_____

Write several related sentences about what part, if any, a religious book has played in the life of you or someone else in your family. If no religious book has played a part in your family's life, write several related sentences about your attitude toward religion.

_____

_____

_____

_____

_____

_____

_____

_____

THE STOP-OUT ROUTE

At present most people's lives are compartmentalized into several roughly labeled segments: education, career, and retirement. A good many experts now feel that the present cycle is not well adapted to the future. It has, in fact, become a time trap, a trap that has brought problems to many people. Consider the technological changes which have resulted in obsolete jobs and in massive layoffs of workers. In addition, education has not fulfilled the objective of reaching all groups with the kinds of learning people need and want, causing campus unrest and the drop-out rate. Also, with the present system, too many retired people suffer the miseries of poverty.

Innovative thinkers have come up with the idea that there should be pathways throughout a person's life whereby he or she can reenter the education–work cycle. One way this could be handled is to allow a student to "stop-out" of school for a time to get work experience in a given field. The student may decide, after practical experience, that a certain career is not for him or her. Then he or she should have the option of returning to school for education in another field. Sometimes middle-aged people find themselves unhappy in the careers they chose as young people. For them, the option of returning to school for education in a new field might be called "career renewal." If this new approach to life periods can be worked out, society stands to gain through a new sense of identification among people now classified as young, middle-aged, and old.

The challenge of financing continuous education must be met if such a program is to work for all groups of people. In Germany, the unemployment insurance fund is used for this purpose, since its use prevents unemployment. The American system, of course, has been to use the unemployment insurance to pay people *after* they're out of work. Perhaps it is time to re-think our system.

In the United States the day may yet come when "stopping out" replaces "dropping out." It's a route that could benefit not only the individual, but society as well.

Writing Practice

Following are two starter sentences. Use them as the topic sentences for two paragraphs, each to contain at least five sentences. You may use information from the preceding report or from your own knowledge. (A topic sentence is a guiding sentence for a paragraph. It states the main idea of the paragraph. All the rest of the sentences in the paragraph relate to it.)

1. "Stopping out" may be a solution to several problems of the conventional system of

    education. _____

    _____

    _____

    _____

    _____

    _____

    _____

    _____

    _____

    _____

2. Career renewal is important in today's world. _____

    _____

    _____

    _____

    _____

    _____

    _____

_____

_____

_____

_____

Write a paragraph of several related sentences about the career or job you are now preparing to pursue.

_____

_____

_____

_____

_____

_____

_____

_____

_____

_____

_____

_____

_____

_____

_____

SCHOLARSHIP VS. SENSE

A LEGEND OF INDIA RETOLD

Long ago there were four friends who lived in a small village in India. Three of the men had become excellent scholars but were sadly lacking in common sense. The fourth man, while he had no use for scholarship, was very sensible.

One of the scholars proposed that the four friends set out in the world to acquire fame and fortune. They agreed to do so and set off, but they had gone only a little way when the eldest scholar objected to the presence of the man with the common sense. "Everybody knows," the eldest scholar said, "that it's impossible to acquire fame and fortune with common sense alone. It simply can't be done without scholarship!"

The second scholar agreed with the eldest, but the third said, "This is no way to treat our old friend. I think he should be allowed to go with us and share in the fame and fortune that will be ours."

So it was agreed, and the four continued their journey. In a short time they came upon the bones of a dead animal. The eldest scholar was delighted. "Here's a perfect opportunity to test our scholarship," he said. "We can use it to bring this poor dead animal back to life." The other scholars were equally delighted. A discussion followed, in which it was decided which one should assemble the skeleton, which one should supply the flesh and blood, and which one should provide the breath of life.

The fourth man, the man of sense, broke into the discussion. "I advise you not to go through with your plan. Can't you see that those are the bones of a lion? If you bring it back to life, it will kill us all."

"What an idiot!" cried one scholar. "How wrong you are!" cried another. The third said, "You stupid man! You are to be pitied for your lack of scholarship."

"Have it your way," muttered the man of sense, and he climbed the nearest tree with all possible speed.

The scholars went about their task of bringing the lion back to life. As soon as the resurrection was accomplished, the lion promptly gobbled them up.

And what happened to the man of sense? He waited until the lion had gone elsewhere, then climbed down from the tree and went, as a sensible man should, home.

Writing Practice

1. Explain in one paragraph of several related sentences the point of this legend.

_____

_____

_____

_____

_____

_____

_____

_____

_____

_____

_____

_____

_____

_____

_____

2. It might be argued that modern human beings have gotten themselves into the situation of the three scholars: their creations may destroy them. Write two or three related paragraphs about one or more creations of man that have the potential to destroy humanity.

_____

_____

_____

_____

_____

THE PEACEFUL POLE

Antarctica may be the world's biggest deep freeze, but that doesn't keep people from visiting or working there. And the desire for an unlimited supply of ice cubes is not what draws them to the land of penguins and seals.

Eleven nations have set up bases for scientific research at the South Pole. Their scientists have been rewarded with much valuable information, some of which could benefit citizens of the Northern Hemisphere. For example, weather conditions originating on Antarctica have great influence on the rest of the world's weather. Careful study of these conditions may someday result in actual weather control. Then there are the coal and minerals of the polar mountains, although as yet no economically feasible way of mining them has been found.

On the recreational side are the cruise ships. They take hardy visitors to polar shores during the summer, when it's wintertime up north. Some farseeing people predict that Antarctica will someday be dotted with ski lodges.

Those who work for the scientific research bases lead lonely, isolated lives during their terms of service. However, they can take pride not only in the importance of their work, but also in the political stance of the eleven nations they represent. These nations have signed a treaty pledging that all their activities in Antarctica will be devoted to peaceful purposes only.

American interest in Antarctica was stimulated by the late Admiral Richard E. Byrd, who began his journeys to "Little America" in December, 1928. Admiral Byrd wrote several books about his explorations, one of them entitled *Little America*.

Probably most people wouldn't care to endure the winters in Antarctica, when the sun disappears for six months and temperatures drop as low as 100 degrees below zero. Most people are probably glad to accept the dedication to scientific research and to peace that prevails there, while remaining in a more comfortable climate somewhere else in the world.

Writing Practice

Answer each of the following questions in a paragraph of at least six related sentences. You may use any general knowledge you have as well as the information in the preceding article.

1.   Why do people want to visit the frigid region of the world called Antarctica?

_____

_____

_____

_____

_____

_____

_____

_____

_____

_____

_____

_____

_____

_____

2.   What sort of lives do those who work in Antarctica lead?

_____

_____

_____

_____

_____

_____

_____

_____

_____

_____

_____

_____

_____

_____

On a separate piece of paper write two paragraphs, one about the advantages of the climate of the area in which you live, the other about the disadvantages. Use as many sentences in each as you think necessary to do a reasonably complete job.

"SUPERSLEUTH": A SUPER PAIN IN THE NECK

New York City had a super problem with parking tickets issued by their super-conscientious law enforcement officers. The problem grew to such fantastic proportions because of the paperwork involved in sending out all those summonses; then, to make matters worse, the city lost super amounts of money when seventy percent of the people ignored their summonses.

City officials were sure they'd found the perfect answer in "Supersleuth," a computer which could match up license numbers on tickets with the names and addresses of the cars' owners. It also could—and did—print out warnings demanding payment of fines.

"Supersleuth" did a terrific job of sending out warnings and bringing in fines. It was even getting lots of fan mail—all of it angry. Unfortunately, "Supersleuth" had developed the super bad habit of sending warning notices to innocent citizens. Even when these indignant people had appealed their notices and had been acquitted, "Supersleuth" continued the barrage of threatening letters.

The blame was refused by "Supersleuth," which shifted it instead to New York's law enforcement officers. It said it couldn't read the license numbers on the tickets because the cops had such super poor handwriting. The cops came back with the lame defense that winter weather froze their ballpoint pens.

The individual made super unhappiest by "Supersleuth" is probably a man from Bethpage, New York. He drove to New York City to protest his warning notice. He won the appeal, all right; but while he was in court, someone stole his car!

Writing Practice

1. On a separate piece of paper, explain in a paragraph or two what "Supersleuth" is, what it was designed to do, and where it went wrong.

2. Assume that you have received a parking ticket through "Supersleuth," that you have never parked at the place you were cited for parking in, that a judge dismissed the charges against you, and that you are still receiving repeated notices from "Supersleuth" to pay the fine or else. On a separate piece of paper, write a letter to the mayor protesting the treatment you have received and demanding that the notices stop.

CHIMPANZEE CHATTER

It has been known for some time that the chimpanzee, among the kinds of mammals living today, comes closest to man in brain structure and reasoning power. A major difference between man and chimp, however, is that the chimp has never developed the power of speech. Apparently, the brain and vocal equipment of the chimpanzee are not adaptable to human speech.

Two psychologists at the University of Nevada decided to try a different approach to the problem of two-way language communication. Using American Sign Language (the hand gestures used by the deaf), they taught a chimp named Washoe a vocabulary of 175 words. At first Washoe learned just the gestures for individual words, mainly those signifying her needs. But in a very short time Washoe was learning to make the signs for every object she was shown and for the names of people around her. Soon after that she showed herself capable of putting together three or four word sentences in answer to questions.

The next step in Washoe's progress is even more remarkable. She voluntarily noted anything that interested her in the world around her: dogs, pigs, trees, flowers. One day when she was with one of the psychologists a plane flew overhead. Washoe looked up, then at the psychologist, and signed: "You me ride plane."

What will the next step be? Will Washoe someday signal, "You me change places"?

Writing Practice

1. On a separate piece of paper, explain in a paragraph or two how the two psychologists mentioned in the preceding anecdote solved the problem of communication between a chimpanzee and men.

2. On a separate piece of paper, explain in a paragraph or two the advantages and disadvantages of sign language as a means of communication. OR Discuss in a paragraph or two the way or ways people communicate with one another without sounds. (Do *not* include sign language in your discussion.)

PLANTS AND ESP

For some years a lie detector specialist has performed experiments which prove to him that plants have reactions to people, to animals, and to threats to their own well-being. This man attaches lie detectors to the leaves of plants; then he watches the signals sent out by the plants and recorded on a polygraph machine (lie detector).

His experiments suggest that plants have a kind of memory. Six of his polygraph students participated in one of his early experiments in which one student, chosen by lot, secretly destroyed a plant. The only witness was another plant. The six suspects were paraded before the surviving plant, which was attached to a polygraph machine. The plant showed no reaction to five of the suspects; but its reaction to the sixth, the one who had destroyed the other plant, as recorded on the machine, were wild.

Other experiments by the lie detector specialist seem to have proved that plants know when their owners like them and are kind to them; they appear to react to praise with healthy growth. On the other hand, says the specialist, plants which are mistreated by their owners or are talked to in an unkind fashion will respond by doing poorly or even dying. A plant in danger may go into a state similar to that of shock in human beings.

The question then arises: do plants sense when they are in danger from humans? For example, when you approach a tomato with a sharp knife, does it know that you are about to slice it into a salad? The lie detector specialist believes that the tomato does know. However, he says, it faints or goes into shock. Presumably this keeps the tomato from realizing its eventual fate!

While the lie detector specialist is not a bona fide scientist, he has been extremely careful to use bona fide scientific methods in his experiments. So far he has received little criticism from scientists about his theories. Perhaps it will have to be left up to the *violette* (violet) or the *dent de lion* (dandelion) to prove or disprove the ESP-in-plants theories of the man with the polygraph machine.

Writing Practice

1. On a separate piece of paper, explain in your own words in two or three paragraphs how the lie detector specialist tried to prove that plants have a sort of ability to feel and react.

2. On a separate piece of paper, write a page or more of the conversation that might go on between two rose bushes who spot a gardener coming toward them with pruning shears. (See the Handbook section for punctuation of dialogue if you don't know how to manage conversation in writing.)

RETIRE TO A REEF

International law says that anyone can claim for himself land which lies above high water. That's exactly what the Ocean Life Research Foundation has done, by planting a flag (a yellow torch of freedom on a blue sea) on some islands of coral and sand that the foundation has built on top of two large coral reefs. Without these islands, the reefs would be submerged at high tide.

The land they have claimed is in the South Pacific Ocean, not far from the islands of Fiji and Tonga. Eventually, the foundation plans to have the land reclaimed and cities built. The name of this new country will be the Republic of Minerva, and it will be somewhat Utopian. A spokesman says the foundation will welcome people who want to get away from taxes, which most people agree are painfully high; from big government, which is dominating many people's lives; and from the terrors of crime.

Because it feels it has a prior claim to the reefs, the kingdom of Tonga is not about to recognize the new republic. Fiji isn't happy about having this new neighbor, either. According to Fiji's prime minister, there are many South Pacific reefs submerged at high tide. And if two such reefs can be claimed for settlement, why couldn't others be claimed also?

It's an idea that might appeal to quite a few people—adventurers, misfits of society, or those who just want to relax. Is anyone interested in retirement on a reef? Applicants are not limited to modern Robinson Crusoes!

Writing Practice

1. The Ocean Life Research Foundation offers life in the Republic of Minerva as an escape from "the terrors of crime." On a separate piece of paper, explain in your own words in two or three paragraphs why you believe that life in Minerva would (or would not) be free from crime.

2. If you were going to live on a small tropical island in the sea and were allowed to take only five items with you, what items would you choose? On separate paper, write several paragraphs explaining what you would take and why you would choose those items. Be sure to relate your paragraphs to each other so that they form one whole, coherent paper.

TATTOO: A PERMANENT STATEMENT

The art of tattooing, an ancient one, is enjoying a comeback, particularly among young women. Why this should be true is debatable. Some people advance the theory that a tattoo is a permanent statement, in contrast to the impermanence of today's society. In a world of shifting values, where people are in danger of losing their identity, they can assert control over their own body by having it tattooed, thus differentiating themselves from the mob. Other people think the tattoo craze is only a passing fad.

There is a third school of thought which states that tattooing, in essence, is sexual: witness the long, sharp needles, the liquid dye poured into the pricked skin, the curious combination of pleasure and pain, and the large number of erotic designs. Natives of several primitive countries tattoo various parts of their bodies to indicate that they are married or wish to be so.

Tattoo parlors in New York City had to go underground when they were outlawed in 1961. The health department claimed that dye solutions and unsterile needles caused an outbreak of serum hepatitis among people who were tattooed. Business in Illinois suffered, too, when the legislature passed a law in 1963 stating that it was illegal to tattoo anyone under twenty-one. One Chicago tattooer, who was in favor of the law, said, "By the time you're twenty-one, you know if you want a tattoo, why you want it, and what you want."

Tattooing apparently began in Egypt as part of the puberty and women's fertility rites. Although Egyptian sailors seem to have spread the custom around the world, tattooing was at first considered almost exclusively a woman's prerogative. Legend has it that the art of tattoo was brought to Samoa by goddesses who swam from Fiji singing, "Tattoo women, not men." Along the way the message was garbled, and the version the goddesses sang on arrival was just the opposite.

Those who wish to be tattooed are advised to think long and hard before they go through with it. A tattoo lasts forever, unless you are prepared to invest a small fortune in a dermatologist and undergo as much pain getting rid of the tattoo as you underwent to get it, or more.

Whether tattooing is primarily sexual in nature, or a fad, or a self-assertive experience, it is a statement. Just what the tattooed person is stating may not always be entirely clear; perhaps it is a kind of link between his or her past and future. Or perhaps it's merely a way of saying, "Look, I'm ME. This proves it."

Writing Practice

1. Tattooing has a long history. Perhaps it will continue to flourish in the future. On separate paper, write a short essay about some possible beneficial uses of tattooing now and in the future. OR Write a short paper about other forms of adornment people use to assert their own individuality.

2. The city council in your town has just banned tattooing within the city limits. You are the editor of a local paper and disagree with that ban. Write an editorial protesting the ban and explaining why it should be repealed.

OLD MAN
AND
OLD WOMAN

AN AMERICAN INDIAN LEGEND RETOLD

A very long time ago there were only two people in the world: Old Man and Old Woman. One day Old Woman said to Old Man, "Come, we must decide something important. How shall we arrange for the people to live when they're on earth?"

"The main thing," said Old Man, "is that I am to have first say about everything."

"Agreed!" said Old Woman. "Only I must have second say."

Old Man began to list the duties of the women. "They shall tan the animals' hides," he said, "and scrape them carefully. The women must do this work quickly, for it will not be hard."

"I can't agree," said Old Woman. "Oh, the women must tan the hides, just as you said. But it must be very hard work."

"All right," said Old Man. "Now, the people shall have faces, with eyes and mouth straight up and down."

"Let's not do it that way," said Old Woman. "Let's have their eyes and mouths crosswise in their faces."

Old Man was becoming annoyed, but he went on to other matters. "The people will have ten fingers on each hand."

"That will never do!" Old Woman exclaimed. "They should have four fingers and one thumb on each hand."

"Hmph!" said Old Man. "All right, if you know so much, what shall we do about life and death? Shall people live forever, or shall they die?"

They argued the subject for a long time. Finally Old Man decided to throw a buffalo chip in the water. If it floated, the people would live forever; if it sank, they'd die forever.

The buffalo chip floated.

"That's no good at all!" Old Woman declared. She threw a rock in the water, saying that if it floated, the people would live forever; if it sank, they'd die forever.

The rock sank.

"That's good," said Old Woman with satisfaction. "People shouldn't live forever. If they did, they wouldn't feel sorry for each other. Nobody would want to help anybody else."

"Oh, all right," said Old Man. "Have it your way."

Then one day Old Woman had a daughter. The baby was sickly and soon died. Old Woman was very sorry that she had thought it a good thing for people to die forever.

"Old Man," she coaxed, "let's have our say over again about life and death."

"No," said Old Man firmly. "We had our say, and we made an agreement. Now we must stick to it."

And ever since that time people have died. In the end, his way was better than hers.

Writing Practice

1. Write a paper about some possible consequences in our society if the average life span, now about seventy years, were only forty years and if it were one hundred years. OR Write a legend or myth which explains the origins of marriage. Try to use some dialogue in your story.

WORK LIKE A DOG? NOT IN THE FUTURE!

We must face the fact that our highly industrialized society is likely to become more, rather than less, industrialized in the future. With this premise is associated the equally likely one that a great many jobs will remain routine and mechanical in nature. It is not a cheering prospect when one considers the large number of people who are already doing work that is dull, tedious, and low paying.

Management and labor experts must find new ways to provide more jobs and to help people to obtain both financial and psychological rewards from their work. Various methods to achieve these goals have been suggested; one plan, in complete contradiction to present practice, is to pay more for routine jobs: those who enjoy their jobs would earn less, while those who must engage in drudgery would earn more.

Other, simpler suggestions are the reduction of hours for routine and mechanical work; rotation of routine, assembly type jobs; and making the job environment more pleasant with attractive physical and social surroundings. A guarantee of job security for unskilled workers is quite the opposite of the present approach, but it would pay off in the long run by protecting people who might otherwise become burdens on society. Beyond that, the lift in the morale of unskilled workers could be tremendous; rather than living in constant fear of losing their jobs, they might begin to take some pride in their work. Going a step further, provisions could be made in even the dull, routine job areas for workers to receive sabbaticals, continuing education, and job-switching help.

But these changes have nothing to do with the nature of work itself and whether it is interesting or dull. The question then arises: how much really interesting work is there in a society which is largely automated?

One answer is that some of the people who are displaced by machines may turn to crafts. Though perhaps not bringing great monetary reward, great satisfaction can be derived from making something with your own hands. Another possibility is the creation of many new, essentially interesting jobs in a field that has so far been largely volunteer—that of "helping people" in schools, playgrounds, hospitals, and daycare centers. Because the psychological rewards are high in such jobs, the salaries could be modest as long as job security was provided.

Another and more radical approach is that of giving workers a financial and satisfaction-producing stake in their jobs. Some companies now provide profit-sharing plans, and some even allow employees a voice in management. But so far, few of those who work at menial, routine jobs have been extended these privileges. The basic idea is that workers who own shares of a company and can vote on management techniques are more likely to take pride in and enjoy their jobs.

An excellent example of such worker participation is the Egged Bus Company in Israel. The employees of this company are among the highest paid in the country, and they all receive similar wages besides sharing in the profits. Not only are the worker's jobs rotated among drivers, mechanics, and dispatchers, but so are the jobs of management.

Even though many people in our society do not desire to be intensely involved in their jobs, preferring instead to find fulfillment through their families or in personal interests, it is surely not too much to ask that most people be able to enjoy whatever it is they do all day. No doubt even a dog would refuse to do some of the boring, tiring, unrewarding jobs that many people are forced to accept!

Writing Practice

Write a paper setting forth in some detail the characteristics of the ideal job for you at the present time and the characteristics of the ideal job for you ten years in the future. OR Write a fanciful account of life in the future when all menial tasks are handled by robots or other machines. What do people do with their time when relieved of hard, tedious, routine work?

OUR FIRST PRESIDENT- JOHN WHO?

There are a group of historians, called Hansonites, who contend that George Washington was not really the first president of the United States. They claim that honor, instead, for one John Hanson, born April 3, 1715, in Charles County, Maryland. The Hansonites base their claim on the fact that their man was a member of the Continental Congress and a signer of the Articles of Confederation. On November 5, 1781, John Hanson was elected President of the Continental Congress. A point the Hansonites consider most significant is the wording of the Articles: "...the Confederation of the United States of America was completed." Therefore, did not that also make John Hanson President of the Confederation of the United States of America? So argue the Hansonites.

Suppose the contention of the Hansonites were to be accepted by Americans in general? Imagine the confusion that would be caused in re-naming all the towns, cities, streets, schools, and parks, to say nothing of the Hanson Senators!

And what would happen to the long-cherished legends associated with George Washington's name? The cherry growers, pickers, and canners would have a problem; for all we know, John Hanson hated cherries. Then there's the bit about George's throwing a silver dollar across the Rappahannock. John may have had no pitching arm at all.

Every red-blooded American knows that George Washington could never tell a lie. But how can we be sure about John Hanson? It's just possible that he wasn't above a little white lie now and then!

No doubt the Hansonites are sincere in their claim. Still, a great deal of confusion will undoubtedly be avoided if we continue to think of our first president as George Washington.

Writing Practice

We have a number of stories about George Washington which are probably mythical rather than true, like the story of the cherry tree. Write a paper in which you make up myths about John Hanson that might serve to increase his fame as an American hero. OR Write a paper of several paragraphs about the probable effects of replacing George Washington with John Hanson as our first president. What differences would that make in our lives?

WRITING GUIDE

Producing correct sentences is important to the process of writing well. The Handbook and many of the exercises for writing practice in Section I may have helped you to write good sentences. However, composing a paper consists of more than just producing a series of correct sentences, as some of the later exercises in Section I may have shown you. Composing a paper involves larger considerations; it involves structuring and developing a series of ideas by means of arrangements of words into sentences, sentences into paragraphs, and paragraphs into papers. The result should be a well ordered structure of enough substance to make an impact.

The process by which we compose a paper begins with the largest consideration rather than the smallest, with the whole paper rather than the word or the sentence. The process may be broken down into three steps: prewriting, writing, and rewriting. Although in actual practice these steps may overlap, for purposes of convenience they may be discussed separately in the order indicated. You will find that the more time and effort you put into the first two steps, especially the first, the less time you will have to spend on the third. Indeed, as you become more and more skillful in planning and writing a paper, you may be able to eliminate the third step almost entirely.

PREWRITING

This step consists of everything you do, all the plans and decisions you make, before you begin the actual writing of the first draft of a paper. Good writing is, in one sense, just the orderly record of good thinking, and it is during the prewriting step that you think out the ideas you want to present, decide about the order of materials, choose an audience, and otherwise prepare to convey information, be-

liefs, opinions, and so on in as clear and forceful a manner as you can.

Choosing a topic

The first choice you will have to make is topic or subject matter. Sometimes someone else will supply this for you, as for instance in an examination or the specific writing assignments in this book. If you have to supply your own topic, you will want to choose one you are interested in; if you don't do that, you will have a very difficult time sustaining your efforts and making an impression on your reader. The worst thing you can do to your readers is to bore them, and that is likely to happen if you choose a topic that doesn't interest you as a writer.

Besides being interested in your topic, you should know something about it or be willing to find out something, or both. Probably interest and information go hand in hand, for we learn about the things that interest us and are usually most interested in the things we know a good deal about. In any case, you must have a body of information about the topic you choose, or you will have nothing to write about. For instance, you may have just visited a zoo and developed a burning interest in koalas. Unless you find out something about them, all you can say is that you like them. Such a statement is hardly enough to sustain interest in your reader. Even if your paper is mainly the airing of an opinion, you will have to have some information to back it up. Interest and information, then, are the basic requirements for the choice of a topic.

You may think that you do not know enough about anything to write a good paper. If that is true, you may have to do a lot of reading and observing; but the chances are it isn't true. You know a great deal about your family and your relationship to other members of it, about school, about your town and neighborhood, maybe about a hobby you follow, certainly about yourself. You have a lot of opinions about a lot of different things, and you probably have reasons for those opinions. You may very well have more trouble deciding which of many possible topics to use than in finding a topic.

Making a statement

Once you have chosen a topic, you must say something about it. For instance, if your topic is drag racing, you need to decide what you want to say about it, since drag racing is such a large topic that you would have to write a book to discuss everything there is to say about it. There are many possibilities for a specific topic for a paper within the general topic of drag racing, like these, for instance:

> To prepare a drag racing car for a race, one must follow certain steps in succession.

> Drag racing has become more and more popular in the last ten years.

> Drag racing should be banned in the United States.

> Some cars are better than others for drag racing.

This process of narrowing and focusing a general topic to one specific statetment allows you to concentrate your thinking on one thing and to ignore everything which would not be relevant to that one main idea.

One way of proceeding in this focusing and narrowing process is to ask yourself a lot of questions. What is drag racing? Why is drag racing popular? What sort of cars hold up best in drag racing? Once you ask yourself enough questions and gather enough answers, you will be able to decide what aspect of drag racing you want to deal with. In doing so you will probably come up with a lot of information, even some that didn't need questions to inspire.

Often one idea sparks another by a process of association. For instance, if someone says "bread," you are likely to think of butter. If someone says "red," you may think of blood. And so on. This process of association can help you to unlock from your memory everything you know about drag racing or any other topic.

However you go about remembering what you know about the topic under consideration, you should jot down all the ideas you have as they occur. Keep on thinking and jotting until you have put down everything you can possibly remember about the topic. Don't try to evaluate or organize the items on your jotted list as you think of them, for that is a different mode of thought and can interfere with the associating function.

Ordering the material

Once you have jotted down everything that you can think of about your topic, you can begin to examine and analyze your material. Out of this examination will come the kind of focusing statement that will form the central point of your paper. For instance, you might decide that you have the most material about the tires that are used in drag races. You could then write a statement something like this: "For a number of reasons, a drag racer operates best with slick tires."

When you have come that far, you are ready to begin organizing your paper. Out of the list of items you have jotted down, you can eliminate any that do not relate to the statement you have decided on. The next step is to arrange the items that do relate in some logical order.

Let's see how this process might develop from the starting point to the final ordering.

The general topic is herbs. I decide that I want to focus on growing herbs in a home garden, since I have been doing that for a number of years and therefore know quite a bit about it and since I am very much interested in home herb gardens. After thinking about the matter for a little while, I produce a guiding statement to help me with my further thinking: "The grower of herbs needs to take into account the type of soil, the amount of water, and the amount of sun when planting his or her herbs." That is a tentative statement which I may want to change later after I have done some jotting and some more thinking. My jotting of bits of information might look like this:

(1) poor soil

(2) self-seed

(3) space

(4) sunlight

(5) gray plants sun

(6) water tolerance

(7) woodruff in shade

(8) buttercup ditto

(9) sorrel needs water

(10) parsley hard to germinate

(11) rosemary little water

(12) ditto thyme

(13) hobby show

(14) southernwood needs room

(15) dill tall

(16) ditto fennel

(17) wormwood big

(18) Job's tears large

(19) pineapple sage spreads

(20) other sages big

(21) creeping thymes

(22) fertilizing unnecessary

(23) trimming

(24) annuals & perennials & biennials

(25) fragrants together

(26) lemon balm & mints shade

(27) mints infest—pennyroyal

(28) bonsai rosemary

(29) oregano infests

(30) marjoram perennial

(31) chives need water, better soil

(32) lavender big

The list could go on, perhaps, but probably I have enough here to get well started. (The numbers in front of the items are for convenience of reference in this book and would not otherwise appear.)

As I examine my list, I find some items that clearly do not belong in my paper, like (13) hobby show and (28) bonsai rosemary. There should be relatively few of these, however, since I was guided in my jottings by a controlling statement to begin with. I notice that other items seem to be closely associated and will probably appear close to one another in the final paper, for instance (1) poor soil and (22) fertilizing unnecessary, and (26) lemon balm & mints shade, (27) mints infest—pennyroyal, and (29) oregano infests. I further notice that I have many items relating to size: (14), (15), (16), (17), (18), (19), (20), (32), so many that I probably need to revise my guiding statement to take this fact into account. The guiding statement now begins to look more like this: "When planning a home herb garden, the grower needs to take into account soil conditions, the amount of space needed for plants, the amount of water needed for proper growth, and the amount of sun needed."

With the new statement in front of me, I can now begin a plan of development. Indeed, there is built right into the statement the beginning of a pattern; my paper will have four main parts: soil, space, water, sun. Now I need to pull all the items into their part or parts of the scheme, and I will be about ready to begin writing.

Under "soil" I will want to include (1) and (22) and perhaps (31). When I put these together, I remember (there's association working again) that I should say something about cultivation, too, in this part of the paper.

Under "space" I will include (3), (14), (15), (16), (17), (18), (19), (20), maybe (23), and (32). In addition, I should deal with (27) and (29) here, since crawling outward is a space consideration as much as growing tall. Probably (21) should go here, too, if anywhere. If (21) belongs here, I should also add camomile, for it too is a creeper. I may want to refine this section further later on. We'll see.

Under "water" I'll put (6), (9), (11), (12), and the mints, which need a lot of water, though that doesn't appear in the jottings list. Again association has helped me to find an important item.

Finally, under "sun" I put (4), (5), (7), (26), and probably a general statement about the importance of sunlight to all growing plants.

I find that I have not used all the items on my list: besides (13) and (28), there are (2), (10), (24), (25), and (30). If they don't fit any of my categories, I can either ignore them, make a new category, or try to use them in some way not yet clear. I need not use them all, of course; the process of preparation includes gathering ideas, selecting from the gathered ideas, arranging the ideas into a plan of de-

velopment, and adding related ideas at any point in the process. As I progress in my writing of the paper, I'll decide what to do with those items, if anything.

Now I have a pretty clear notion of what points I will make in my paper, for I have arranged all my information into four groups. All I need to decide is the order of presentation of the groups. Soil, sun, water, space? Space, soil, water, sun? Something else? I decide that soil, space, sun, water seems sensible, though I wouldn't feel uncomfortable with some other ordering.

So I have, in effect, created a functional outline (dreaded word!) by examining the material and then finding the best form for the presentation of that material. In its simplest form it will look like this:

Soil

Space

Sun

Water

I can put this into a more or less standard form if I like, with some of the subheadings implied in earlier thinking:

I. Soil

  A. Poor

  B. Unfertilized

  C. Cultivated

II. Space

  A. Tall and bushy

  B. Infestive

  C. Creeping

III. Sun

  A. Full or nearly full sun

  B. Shade or little sun

IV. Water

    A. Little

    B. Much

If I wanted to, I might go even further and include in my outline the numbers from my list to indicate what specific content will be. For instance, for II B I might note (6) water tolerance, (9) sorrel, (31) chives, and mints. However, I probably won't do that, for I can remember most of the information on the list and can refer to it if I need to; and I am not really interested in perfecting an outline, but in writing a paper. The outline is only a means to that end.

It is, of course, a very important means, really indispensable for most writers and for all beginning writers. The outline performs several important functions. First, it forces writers to think in an orderly fashion, or at any rate to record the results of their thinking in an orderly way, reflecting the decisions they make as they go along. Second, it allows an overview of the structure of the paper before the paper is written. It is like looking at the blueprint of a house in order to make sure that all the rooms are in the right relationships to one another. Making changes in a blueprint to reflect changes in intention is a good deal easier than rebuilding the house after it is finished. So with a paper; it is easier to rearrange the items in an outline than to rewrite the whole paper after it is finished. Finally, the outline permits the writer to concentrate on one thing at a time during the writing process. Trying to decide what to say in the second part while writing the first part interferes with the attention necessary for effective sentence and paragraph formation. Since the outline already records what is to come next, the writer can concentrate on what he or she is doing at each point along the way as he or she progresses from the beginning to the end of the paper.

The outline is not sacred, of course. If a writer thinks of a new idea or arrangement of material as the paper is progressing, the new thought should be welcomed. If it means stopping the process and returning to the outline, that should be done. The writer must be careful, however, not to include new ideas without considering the whole outline. Maybe the new idea won't really fit. The important thing to consider is the outline of the whole paper and how everything should fit together to get across the main idea.

WRITING

With my outline now well in hand, I am almost ready to begin writing my first draft. But first I must consider my introduction. I didn't include that in my outline making, for I knew that I would have to have one; every paper has to have some way to get started. I remember the familiar pattern—introduction, body, conclusion. So far I have been concerned with the body, the part with all the substance in it. My outline reflects only that. Now I must turn my attention to finding a good opening for my paper.

Introduction

What should I put into it? The introduction must serve the function of letting the reader know right away what the paper is about, so I must include my guiding statement in some form. Since it was a useful guide to me in putting my outline together, it will probably be useful to the reader in reading what I have to say. I should try to capture the reader's attention, too, so that the person who is reading my paper will want to find out more about my subject. Maybe I will need to supply some background material as well, like definitions of terms or a statement of my qualifications to write about herbs. I should, in short, include anything that will engage the reader's interest and help make clear what I have to say. I need to write the introduction with special care, for it is the first thing the reader sees.

So I write this as my introduction.

We have recently witnessed a revival of interest in herbs, perhaps as one consequence of the back-to-the-land movement. Magazines like *Sunset* have featured stories, with many pictures, about herbs, and dozens of books have been published in the last five years about using and growing herbs. Many of the stories and books assert that growing herbs in the home garden is relatively easy; and as an herb gardener on a restricted city lot, I agree. I have had good success with little experience and no training. I have found, however, that I do need to take several factors into account if I am to get the best results from my time and effort.

That isn't exactly exciting as an opening, but it's probably interesting enough to make the reader want to go on. It does give certain useful information, like my qualification to write on the topic. Most important of all, it suggests, at the end of the paragraph, what the paper intends to do; it will talk about "several factors" that are important in growing herbs.

Body

The developing paragraphs that make up the body of my paper will follow along the sequence indicated by the outline. Each one will contain a good deal of specific information, the items I jotted down on my initial list and then arranged into the outline. All or most of the paragraphs will follow a fairly similar form and will exhibit certain common characteristics. (Further information about developing paragraphs will appear a bit later in this section.)

The first developing paragraph I write, the one right after the introduction, turns out like this:

The first consideration is soil. Unlike most vegetables and flowers, herbs seem to prefer poor soil, or at least thrive on it. Perhaps this is so because many of them were originally weeds and have not been hybridized and "improved", as many other plants have. Though they will grow in enriched soil, they lose some of their better qualities when they do. For instance, the fragrant geraniums, like *pelargonium graveolens*, the rose geranium, grow so fast in fertilized soil that they produce less of the essential oils that make them so fragrant. Consequently I do not use steer manure or (heaven forbid!) chemical fertilizers on my herbs. All I do is cultivate the soil from time to time to allow for better water absorption and once in a while add some mulch or compost to lighten the texture of the soil. I conclude that I am doing something right, for my herbs grow vigorously.

Then I go on to each of the other developing paragraphs in turn, using my outline as a guide. I incorporate the relevant information from my earlier lists and add any other that is clearly appropriate as I fashion the successive paragraphs. When I am finished with my last one, I am almost through with my first draft. All that is left is the ending.

Conclusion

The purpose of the conclusion is to round off the paper, to provide a sense of closure. I should indicate in my ending that I have finished what I set out to do. I may want to summarize, though in a short paper that would be unnecessary, and I certainly will want to emphasize the main point of my paper, the one I set forth by implication in the opening.

Knowing all that, I compose my conclusion:

I'm pleased with my herb garden. I urge anyone interested in growing things to try a few herbs. They're sure to bring satisfaction, and they're easy to grow. Even without knowledge of their preferences in soil, space, sun, and water, new herb growers can probably get the kind of results that will make them pleased with their herb gardens, too.

That says a pleasant goodbye to the reader, emphasizes the factors to be considered in the growing of herbs, and brings the paper to a comfortable close. I am now finished except for whatever revisions I want to make as I reread the paper in preparation for the final draft. (Hints on revision appear later in this section.)

Paragraphs

A word about paragraphs before we go on to a discussion of rewriting. As we have seen, the introductory paragraph (an introduction may of course have more than one paragraph) has a special function and therefore takes a special form different from that of developing paragraphs. Usually the introductory paragraph leads from a fairly general statement to a specific statement of its intention, which is usually the last sentence. The introductory paragraph contains no developing material; that is left to the developing paragraphs.

The concluding paragraph also has a special function, to bring the paper to a close. It may take a number of forms, whatever is appropriate to the paper of which it is a part. It will not contain developing materials, though, and will introduce no new ideas.

The rest of the paragraphs in a paper will be developing paragraphs. They fulfill the contract made in the introduction by bringing together information in an orderly fashion, as we have seen in the paragraph on soil. The effectiveness of a paper depends mostly upon the quality of its developing paragraphs. If they are too skimpy or if they are confused, the paper cannot make its point.

Most developing paragraphs follow a standard strategy: they begin with a *topic sentence*, a guiding sentence for all that is to follow, much like the guiding sentence in an introduction that controls the rest of the paper that is to follow. There are exceptions to this practice, but you will never go wrong if you open a paragraph with its topic sentence. Let's see how this works with the paragraph indicated in the outline as III A:

Besides space, most herbs, like a majority of other plants, need to be in the direct rays of the sun for at least a part of every day. All of the gray-foliaged herbs, for instance wormwood, gray santolina, and lavender, must have a good deal of sunlight. Dill, fennel, the sages, rosemary, thyme, and marjoram all grow best in the sun. Chives need at least partial sun, as do fragrant-leaved geraniums. If I am in doubt about a plant's preference, I always put it where it can get a lot of sun, and I'm seldom disappointed with the results.

In this paragraph the first sentence is the topic sentence; it announces what the paragraph will be about, the need of herbs for sun. All the rest of the sentences deal in specific detail with herbs that thrive best in the sun. The rest of the paragraphs in the paper about herbs follow the same strategy. (The full paper appears at the end of this section.)

In addition to a common strategy, developing paragraphs usually display three common characteristics: completeness, coherence, and unity. How complete should a paragraph be? There is no single answer to that question, of course, but a paragraph should contain enough substance (it is substance, not just length, that counts) to make an impact and to make an adequate contribution to the paper of which it is a part. Few paragraphs can be effective with fewer than three or four sentences. If paragraphs get too long, of course, they may have to be broken into two or more parts for purposes of convenience. That seldom happens, though. Paragraphs are more likely to be too short than too long.

A paragraph is said to be coherent when it flows smoothly, when each of the sentences in it relates clearly to its neighbors and the progression is plain. Coherence is achieved mostly by careful planning; a workmanlike writer composes in coherent sequences. However, relationships may be emphasized and readers given extra help by transitional words, by the repetition of words or phrases, or by other means. (See p. 347 in the Handbook for more on transitions.)

Unity means that everything in the paragraph pertains to the same topic, the one announced in the topic sentence. All the details in a paragraph should relate directly to the point the paragraph is making.

The paragraph indicated by IV A B in the outline will illustrate all of these characteristics. (Note that in the writing I combined into one paragraph what I had expected to be two when I prepared the outline.)

Water is of course a necessity for all growing plants. Though many herbs are fairly tolerant, surviving both wet and dry conditions, some prefer little water, some a lot. Rosemary, lavender, the thymes, dittany of Crete, fringed wormwood, and Mexican sage can go thirsty for a long time if the weather is not blisteringly hot. On the other hand, sorrel demands generous drinks of water frequently. Chives (like most members of the onion family), pennyroyal, and the mints are all hearty drinkers; mint grows well even when constantly wet beneath the drip of a hose connection. The rest of the herbs, like marjoram, oregano, parsley, and rue, need amounts of water somewhere in between little and much. Since I cannot always take the time to allot the water properly to each plant but instead water them all alike, I probably don't get the best out of all of them. However, I seldom lose one, so I guess they can all adapt as they need to.

The first sentence sets forth the topic, the necessity for water for plants, including herbs. The second sentence expands on the idea, indicating that some herbs take little water, some a lot. Then comes, logically, a list of dry-tolerant herbs. "On the other hand" signals a change of direction; after the phrase comes a list of water-loving plants, with a special reference to mints. Finally, the paragraph mentions some herbs that take moderate amounts of water, a logical progression after those which take a little and a lot. The paragraph concludes with a reference to my watering practices.

Everything in the paragraph pertains to its topic—unity. It has enough substance to make its point—completeness. It holds together as a smooth, related sequence of sentences with transitions where necessary—coherence. It therefore demonstrates the strategy of the topic sentence and supporting sentences and the three qualities of good developing paragraphs.

In addition, the paper as a whole displays the same general form and qualities. It has a guiding statement, it is complete enough to do the job it sets out to do, it has no extraneous material, and it all holds together in a tight structure.

I am ready now to undertake any revisions that may be necessary or desirable.

REWRITING

If I have planned carefully, gathering as much material as possible about my topic and ordering it logically by means of a sound outline, and if I have followed that outline as I constructed my paragraphs and sentences, I should have little need for rewriting (revision is another term for the same process). However, almost every paper can profit from close scrutiny after it is written, for in the process of writing things can go wrong that we are not aware of while we are busy with the actual composition of the paper. If I read my own paper as if someone else had written it, I may find that some sentences that seemed entirely clear to me when I wrote them are a little vague or confusing to me now, as a reader. I may discover faulty punctuation, a misspelling or two, an awkward sentence, or a wrong word choice.

One way to proceed in the critical reading that is essential to revision is to ask a series of questions. Depending upon the answers we give, we will have to do a lot of revision or only a little. For instance, if my answer to the first of the following questions is no, I will have to start all over again. Some of the other questions imply only a bit of tidying up here and there. Here is the list of questions.

1. Do I have enough information on my topic? If not, could I get more? Does the paper seem weak because it has too little substance?
2. Does my paper have a sound structure? Is it arranged in such a way that the reader can follow it easily throughout? Do the parts relate logically to the whole?
3. Does the introduction state or imply clearly what the paper is about? Does it give the reader a start in the right direction?
4. Does each of the developing paragraphs have sufficient substance? Is each unified and coherent? Does each relate clearly to the others?
5. Are all of the sentences correct and clear? Have I used conventional punctuation in all of them? Have I spelled the words right?
6. Does my conclusion satisfactorily bring my paper to a close, giving the reader the sense that I have finished what I set out to do? Have I remembered to emphasize the main point of my paper in the conclusion?

As I read my paper through, answering the questions as I go, I can make whatever changes seem necessary. I may have to make only a few corrections in spelling; I may have to reword sentences; I may have to rearrange the sentences in a paragraph or add more sentences to create more substance; or I may have to tear up the paper and start over. In any case, the rewriting that I do will make my paper clearer, smoother, and more persuasive.

Somewhere in this sequence of prewriting, writing, and rewriting I must decide on a title. This is more difficult than it seems. I will want something fairly short, no more than four or five words; I will want something which will help to guide the reader by suggesting accurately what the paper is about; and I will want something that is intriguing enough to catch my reader's interest. I will probably not want a full sentence, only a phrase. After considerable deliberation, I decide to title my paper "Putting Herbs in Their Places." That seems to satisfy all the requirements for a title.

Now all that is left is to prepare the final draft. If I write it in longhand, I will write legibly, in ink, on every other line, leaving margins of an inch or so on left and right, and I will use only one side of the paper. If I type, I will double space, leaving fifteen-space margins on left and right, and will use only one side of the paper.

I will then sigh in relief and submit my paper proudly, aware that I have done the best job of writing I could do.

Writing Practice

1. Following is the complete text of "Putting Herbs in Their Places." Using the six questions on p. 79 as a guide, analyze the paper thoroughly, showing how it meets the requirements of the writing principles discussed in this section.

2. Choose a topic you are interested in and know a lot about. Go through the prewriting, writing, and rewriting processes discussed in this section and construct a complete, coherent, unified, and interesting paper on that topic. Be prepared to submit to your instructor the material that shows that you have gone through the entire process: narrowing a general subject to a specific topic; your first topic statement; the jottings of all the ideas you have had about the topic; the groupings of the ideas in your jottings; the revised guiding statement, if you needed to revise it; your outline; your first draft of the paper; and your revised final draft.

Putting Herbs in Their Places

We have recently witnessed a revival of interest in herbs, perhaps as one consequence of the back-to-the-land movement. Magazines like *Sunset* have featured stories, with many pictures, about herbs; and dozens of books have been published in the last five years about using and growing herbs. Many of the stories and books assert that growing herbs in the home garden is relatively easy, and as an herb gardener on a restricted city lot, I agree. I have had good success with little experience and no training. I have found, however, that I do need to take several factors into account if I am to get the best results from my time and effort.

The first consideration is soil. Unlike most vegetables and flowers, herbs seem to prefer poor soil, or at any rate thrive in it. Perhaps this is so because many of them were originally weeds and have not been hybridized and "improved," as many other plants have. Though they will grow in enriched soil, they lose some of their better qualities when they do. For instance, the fragrant geraniums, like *pelargonium graveolens*, the rose geranium, grow so fast in fertilized soil that they produce less of the essential oils that make them so fragrant. Consequently I do not use steer manure or (heaven forbid!) chemical fertilizers on my herbs. All I do is cultivate the soil from time to time to allow for better water absorption and once in a while add some mulch or compost to lighten the texture of the soil. I conclude that I am doing something right, for my herbs grow vigorously.

Though herbs do not need rich soil, they do need considerable space. At first I planted things much too close together, for the small plants I grew from seed or got from the nursery seemed very lonely when set out at the intervals recommended by the books I read. But the books were right: some of my lonesome friends grew four or five feet tall and five or six across. Southernwood, wormwood, Job's tears, pineapple sage, Cleveland sage, fennel, and lavender all surprised me by becoming far too big for the space I had allotted. Fortunately, they didn't mind rather severe trimming, so I could prevent them from killing out the plants they towered over until I could find time to transplant them or root them out and start over, as I had to do with my prize wormwood. Now I know enough, usually, to allow plenty of space for my specimens.

Instead of allowing all the space they want, I restrict some sorts of herbs by keeping them in tubs or pots or by erecting barriers of wood, brick, or concrete. These are the infestive herbs which spread by runners in every direction and can kill anything they invade. Pennyroyal, spearmint, orange bergamot mint, lemon balm, and oregano are examples of herbs with this invasive habit. Costmary does the same thing but at a slower pace.

Other creeping plants I don't try to control, for they make a good ground cover over bare spots and under larger plants. They are not invasive and will not kill other plants. Camomile is such a ground cover. Two kinds of thyme, white moss trailing thyme and caraway thyme, are others. Neither gets much over an inch high, and they spread quickly over a large territory, unlike most thymes, which grow to be small bushes. I particularly like caraway thyme for the fragrance (caraway, of course) which it releases when I walk on it.

Besides space, most herbs, like a majority of other plants, need to be in the direct rays of the sun for at least a part of every day. All of the gray-foliaged herbs, for instance wormwood, gray santolina, and lavender, must have a good deal of sunlight. Dill, fennel, the sages, rosemary, thyme, and marjoram all grow best in the sun. Chives need at least partial sun, as do fragrant-leaved geraniums. If I am in doubt about a plant's preference, I always put it where it can get a lot of sun, and I'm seldom disappointed with the results.

I have discovered, however, that a few herbs demand shade or partial shade. All of the mints I have tried—spearmint, orange bergamot mint, black peppermint—except licorice mint grow best in the shade or partial shade. In fact, too much direct sun kills them. Lemon balm, a close relation to the mints, likes a shady spot, along with pennyroyal, woodruff, and angelica. Job's tears can manage nicely in partial shade.

Water is of course a necessity for all growing plants. Though many herbs are fairly tolerant, surviving both wet and dry conditions, some prefer little water, some a lot. Rosemary, lavender, the thymes, dittany of Crete, fringed wormwood, and Mexican sage can go thirsty for a long time if the weather is not blisteringly hot. On the other hand, sorrel demands generous drinks of water frequently. Chives (like most members of the onion family), pennyroyal, and the mints are all hearty drinkers; mint grows well even when constantly wet beneath the drip of a hose connection. The rest of the herbs, like marjoram, oregano, parsley, and rue, need amounts of water somewhere in between little and much. Since I cannot always take the time to allot the water properly to each plant but instead water them all alike, I probably don't get the best out of all of them. However, I seldom lose one, so I guess they can all adapt as they need to.

I'm pleased with my herb garden. I urge anyone interested in growing things to try a few herbs. They're sure to bring satisfaction and they're easy to grow. Even without knowledge of their preferences in soil, space, sun, and water, new herb growers can probably get the kind of results that will make them pleased with their herb gardens, too.

PICTURES FOR WRITING PRACTICE

INTRODUCTION

In this section are fifteen units, each consisting of a picture or pictures and two related writing activities. Careful study of the pictures may reveal more than you thought was there at first glance. Close observation is as much a thinking process as a seeing process. You may find it useful to discuss what you think you see in a picture with others who may think they see something else.

Although the writing tasks in this section are more complicated and demanding than those in the first section, you should be able to accomplish them after your earlier practice. Each of the assignments contains some suggestions to help you with the writing task proposed. Like the assignments in the first section, those in this section proceed from easy to harder. All of them require that you do some thinking as well as careful observing.

At the end of the section are ten pictures without any writing assignments. They may be assigned by your instructor for supplementary writing. If not, you may want to use them as a basis for discussion with your classmates or for extra writing practice on your own.

Now, start, see, think, and write.

Photography of H. Armstrong Roberts

Writing Practice 1

Study carefully the photograph at the left. Even though you may not understand exactly what is going on, you can observe many details and record them. Notice both what is in the picture and how the various things in it relate to one another.

After you have studied the photograph carefully, write several paragraphs about *what you see* in it. Refer back to the photograph as you go along. Do not try to guess why the figures in the picture are doing what they are doing; just report what is there. Be sure to impose some sort of orderly pattern on your paper. Random observations won't be very effective.

Writing Practice 1a

Ask a friend who has not seen the photograph at the left to make a rough sketch of it from your description written for the assignment above. Your friend does not need to be an artist to do this satisfactorily. (Maybe you could have several friends do this for you; then compare the results.)

When you get the sketch or sketches, compare them with the photograph. Then rewrite your description, taking into account what you may have written inaccurately or vaguely, or what you may have left out the first time you described the photograph. You may also refer to the photo again, of course.

87

Writing Practice 2

Look at the photograph on the facing page. You see certain things in it that you could report accurately so that others could create the scene in their mind's eye: a little boy, an open cupboard, a chair, etc.

This time you are to do more than just describe the scene. Using what you see in the photograph as clues, write several paragraphs about what you think the situation in the photograph is. Do not make up any facts that are not in the picture, but interpret sensibly what is there. Be sure to tie your conclusions to the evidence in the picture which led you to them. You will start with what you see, and then you will build upon that observation, coming to whatever conclusions your understanding of what you see lead you to.

Writing Practice 2a

Rewrite your paper from the assignment above, this time coming to different conclusions from the same evidence. How else might you have interpreted what you saw?

You might want to compare your paper with the papers of some of your classmates. The first papers of all of you may be quite a bit alike. However, there should be considerable variety in the second ones.

Photo courtesy Oliver Johnson

Writing Practice 3

This picture is a scene from a continuing action, something like a single frame from a movie. Write several paragraphs explaining what the action is, where it is taking place, when it is occurring, and whatever else you can think of from the clues given in the photograph and from whatever you may know about this activity. Discuss what the person who is hang gliding might be feeling at this moment and what his motivation for participating in this sport might be.

Writing Practice 3a

Discuss your favorite sport (either one in which you like to participate or one you like to watch). Why is it your favorite? What do you like so much about it? What kind of feelings do you get when you are either participating in it or watching it? Try to interest your reader in this sport enough so that he or she might want to try it, by using precise, vivid language and the right words to convey your own enthusiasm.

Photo courtesy Joan Roloff

Writing Practice 4

On the facing page are two pictures. One is a standard photograph, with considerable detail. The other is a photograph printed in a special way which leaves out much of the detail.

If you saw the second picture without the first, you would still be able to tell what it is. Write a paragraph or more explaining the features of the second which make it recognizable and indicating what has been left out in comparison to the first. Draw any conclusions you can about what is necessary for recognition of objects. Does more detail always make an object more recognizable? Detail *can* add to the visual impact of a picture. Does it always add, or are there times when a more simplified picture is more effective? Which is the more effective picture of an eye, in this case?

Writing Practice 4a

Write several paragraphs explaining what features are necessary for identification of some class of objects of your own choosing and what further details are necessary to make distinctions between individuals within that class. For instance, what features would you have to know to distinguish the class of cows as different from horses? Then what details would you need to tell one kind of cow from another, say Holstein from Hereford? And what other details would you need to tell Old Bessie and Nelliebelle, both Jerseys, from one another?

Photography of H. Armstrong Roberts

Photography of H. Armstrong Roberts

Writing Practice 5

Here you see three photographs with the same central content, hands. Observing the hands in as much detail as you can, write several paragraphs of comparison and contrast about them. Remember that *comparison* is showing how two or more things are alike; *contrast* is showing how things are different. So in this paper you will show in what ways the hands are similar and in what ways they are different. Work out a careful scheme for the presentation of your findings; just a random listing won't be very interesting.

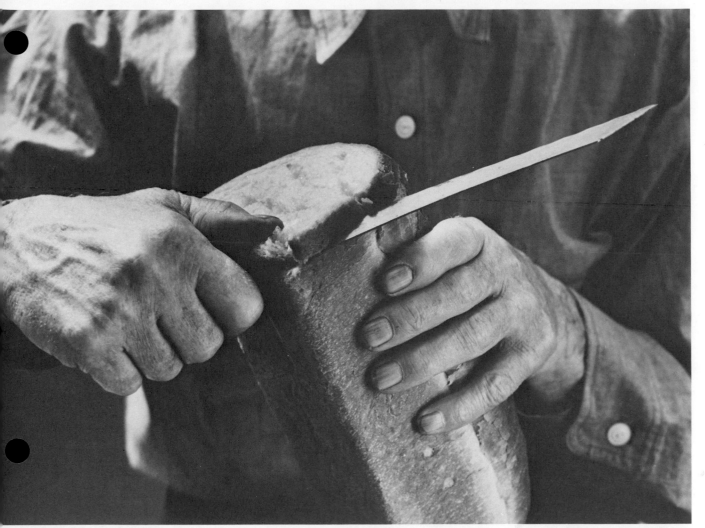

Photography of H. Armstrong Roberts

Writing Practice 5a

Write a comparison and contrast theme using your parents or a couple
of your friends as subjects. Try to deal with personality traits and
character features more than with surface likenesses and differences.
(Everybody already knows that your mother and father are of different
sexes, for instance.) You might want to compare and contrast
backgrounds, too, since what we are like grows out of what we once
were and where we came from. Be as specific as you can, citing details
to back up your statements. Look especially for unusual features about
your subjects, features that will emphasize the individuality of the
people you are writing about.

Writing Practice 6

Study this split picture. Then write a comparison and contrast theme on the content of the picture. You may choose to write about what the wagon and the cars represent as well as what they look like. Keep in mind the background as well as the foreground.

Writing Practice 6a

Write a theme about which of two or more products of the same kind you would buy and why. Would you choose a Ford over a Chevrolet, for instance? A Harmon-Kardon tuner over a Fisher or a Scott? Be sure to discuss the advantages and disadvantages of the products you consider. If you do not know enough about any product to come to a wise decision, perhaps you should go on a shopping expedition for some product you might really buy, just to see how various brands differ.

Writing Practice 7

After studying this photograph, write as complete a word portrait of the man as you can, interpreting whatever clues you can find. Take into account dress, surroundings, facial expression, body position, and anything else that might help you to determine age, occupation, social status, personality, and other characteristics. In other words, in addition to telling what the figure looks like, try to tell what kind of person he probably is.

Compare your portrait with those your classmates write. No doubt some of them will be different from yours. That may indicate something about first impressions (or, in this case, only impressions).

Writing Practice 7a

Sit in front of a large mirror in a pose characteristic of you, dressed in the kind of clothing you usually wear. Maybe you will want to have a cup of coffee or a coke in front of you, or something else characteristic of your own life style. Look at yourself in the mirror for several minutes, trying to observe about yourself the same things you observed about the man in the assignment above. Then write a word portrait about yourself, using as clues only what you see in the mirror. What kind of a person might you be in the eyes of others?

Photography of H. Armstrong Roberts

Photography of H. Armstrong Roberts

Writing Practice 8

The woman in this photograph is showing someone else how to do something, in this case how to make a vase on a potter's wheel. She is able to explain the process as she goes along; perhaps she has been explaining it to the girl who is watching her; if so, the explanation is a lot easier because she can also *show* the other person what she is doing.

Sometimes we can't show people how to do things; we have to tell them, using only the written word or pictures or diagrams. That isn't as effective as showing them, but often it is the best we can do.

Write instructions on how to do something or make something. You need to choose a process that you know well. You may use whatever sketches or diagrams you like to accompany your words. You will probably want to break the process down into simple steps and explain each in turn. Supply enough detail so that someone unfamiliar with the process can do what you want him or her to do.

Writing Practice 8a

The assignment above asked you to write instructions so that someone reading them could do what you wanted done. It was a "how to do it" problem. This assignment asks that you *explain* some process, not give instructions. Your paper should tell what goes on in the manufacture of a product, for instance steel or lumber, but it should not instruct someone in how to go about manufacturing that product. This is a "how it is done" or "how it works" problem. You might want to explain how some action is carried out, like how the state legislature passes a bill. You will probably want to choose a more complex process and break it into larger steps, with less detail, than you did in the first assignment. Your explanation should be complete enough, though, so that a reader will be fairly familiar with the overall process when he or she finishes reading your explanation.

Photo courtesy David K. Johnson

Writing Practice 9

Examine this "double portrait," of a person of college age and a person a generation older. Write a dialogue of at least a couple of pages in which these two people talk to each other about some topic important to both of them (you choose the topic). You may assume any relationship between the two people that will help you write a good paper: father-son, teacher-pupil, family friends, co-workers, etc.

Try to make the dialogue believable, and use quotation marks carefully and correctly. (See rule 18 in the Handbook.)

Writing Practice 9a

Write another paper of two or more pages in which *you* carry on a conversation with one or both of these people, on a topic different from the one you chose for the first paper. Again, assume any relationship that is useful to you.

Compare the two papers you have written. Did your practice in using dialogue in the first paper help you make your second dialogue paper more realistic?

Photography of H. Armstrong Roberts

Writing Practice 10

In the bottle in this photograph is a note, written by someone somewhere and launched upon the waves to seek a far-off shore. The note is two pages of very closely written prose.

What does the note say? Using your imagination freely, write what you think the note says. Make your note a couple of pages long.

Writing Practice 10a

Get from your teacher the note that someone else wrote for assignment 10 and write an appropriate response. Make your response three pages long. (Don't put it in a bottle and send it to sea, though. That would clutter up the ocean and beaches too much.)

Writing Practice 11

On the preceding two pages is a collage of photographs suggesting some of the problems that face us today: racial inequality, exploding populations, poverty, pollution, ineffective education, the significance of religion in modern society, old age, marriage versus new life styles, and so on. Choose one of the problems suggested by the collage or some other important social problem and write a theme persuading someone to your particular point of view on the subject you choose.

This means that you must state a proposition and then support it by whatever means you can. Your theme is more than explanatory: it is also argumentative. For instance, you should not say only that the population of the world is growing at a tremendous rate; you should state a point of view about population growth—that the world should turn its attention to curbing population growth at all costs because if we don't we will eventually destroy the earth, or that scientists will figure out a way for man to continue to exist no matter how much the population grows, or that we should do nothing to tamper with the progress of nature, or some other point of view. Be sure that you have sound reasons for the point of view you state, and be sure you explain those reasons clearly. You are to try to persuade someone that your view is the right one and get your reader to agree with you or even to act in ways that you suggest.

Pages 106–107:
TOP: Photography of H. Armstrong Roberts; Photo courtesy Mark Allen; Photography of H. Armstrong Roberts; Photo courtesy Robert Wylder.
BOTTOM: Photo courtesy Douglas Johnson; Photography of H. Armstrong Roberts; Photography of H. Armstrong Roberts; Photo courtesy Oliver Johnson.

Writing Practice 11a

Although you may be thoroughly convinced that your view on the subject you chose in assignment 11 is the right one, you will no doubt admit that other views are possible and that other people have other ideas.

Write a theme arguing the opposite point of view from the one you took in assignment 11. Try to be just as persuasive in this theme as in the other. If necessary, take time to really investigate this opposing point of view.

When you finish, you might ask yourself whether you are as sure about the subject you chose as you were when you began assignment 11. Sometimes when we thoroughly investigate a point of view the opposite of our own on a controversial subject, we become even more convinced we were right in the first place. Sometimes, on the other hand, we find ourselves less sure of our original point of view. It might be interesting for the class to share with each other what has happened to their points of view during this assignment, and why.

Photo courtesy Oliver Johnson

Photography of H. Armstrong Roberts

Photography of H. Armstrong Roberts

Writing Practice 12

The three children in these photographs are all Americans, born in the land which supposedly provides equal opportunity for all. They all started out equal, at any rate, coming naked and squalling into the world.

Write a theme about the contrasting lives these children will probably lead until age 21, commenting finally upon the equality of their opportunity.

Writing Practice 12a

Write a theme telling about some incident of racial discrimination or inequality of opportunity that you know about from your own experience or from your reading. Use as many specific details as you can.

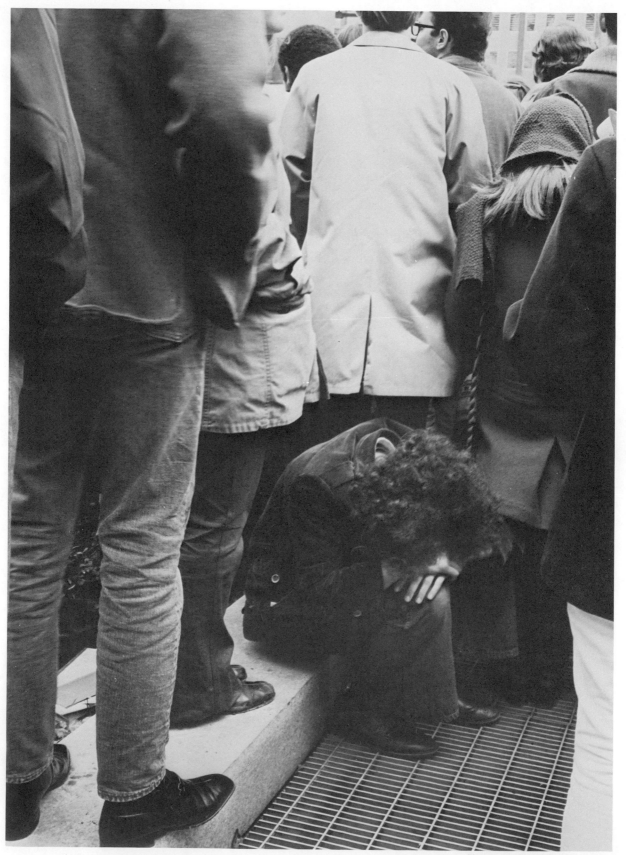

Photography of H. Armstrong Roberts

Writing Practice 13

Notice the slumped figure in this photograph. Write a story using that figure as the central character and the scene in the photo as one of the incidents, if not the central incident, of the story. Except for those limitations, you may use your imagination as freely as you like, inventing whatever characters and incidents you need to suit your purposes. Don't worry too much about a carefully constructed plot, but do create believable characters acting in believable ways.

Writing Practice 13a

Write a story stemming from some incident in your own life. You need not stick to the facts as you remember them; you can expand your experience through your imagination as much as you like. Or you may stick close to what really happened if you want to. In either case, above all else be as specific as possible: use vivid details so the reader can visualize what's happening; try to use fresh combinations of words rather than clichés; have your story move along quite rapidly.

Photography of H. Armstrong Roberts

Writing Practice 14

The figure in this photograph makes a sort of statement. The figure is a symbol, that is, something that stands for something else.

Write a theme explaining what you think the figure stands for and what sort of statement the picture makes: what is the idea it is trying to get across?

Writing Practice 14a

Discuss in a short theme how some of the things in our everyday life may be considered a symbol of something else. For instance, the Cadillac is a symbol of the life of the rich. Even though we know that some people who drive Cadillacs are not rich, many of us still think of rich people when we see Cadillacs. What symbol or symbols mean something to you? Can you always analyze why these particular things are symbolic for you?

Photography of H. Armstrong Roberts

Writing Practice 15

Look at the figure on the facing page. Don't try to determine what it represents, if anything. Just look at it for a while, noting the interconnections, the textures, the light and shadow.

Do you find it interesting? annoying? exciting? dull? frustrating? pleasing? Do you like it? dislike it? feel indifferent to it? Does it remind you of anything?

Write an unstructured paper of a couple of pages setting forth your reactions to the figure. Don't worry about order and paragraphs and such matters. Just get down as many sentences of honest reaction as you can. Feel free to express yourself however you like.

When you are finished, don't share your paper with anyone else if you don't want to. This is your own private thing. Even your teacher shouldn't read it if you don't want him or her to.

Writing Practice 15a

Evaluate the assignments you have done in this section. Which one or ones did you think the most interesting, the most useful, the hardest, and so on? Write a theme setting forth in as orderly a manner as you can your evaluation of the writing experiences growing out of the assignments you were asked to do.

GALLERY: MORE PICTURES

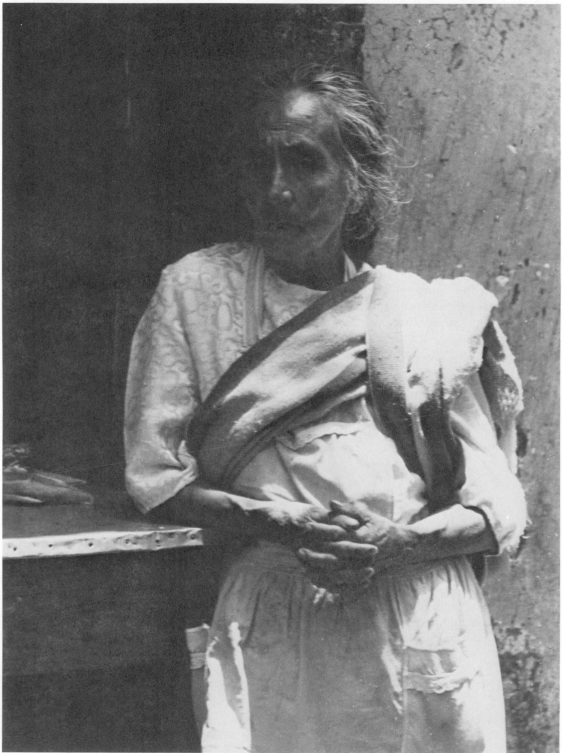

Photo courtesy Oliver Johnson

FOR WRITING PRACTICE

Photography of H. Armstrong Roberts

Photography of H. Armstrong Roberts

Photo courtesy Oliver Johnson

Photo courtesy Ronald A. Oriti

124

Photo courtesy Oliver Johnson

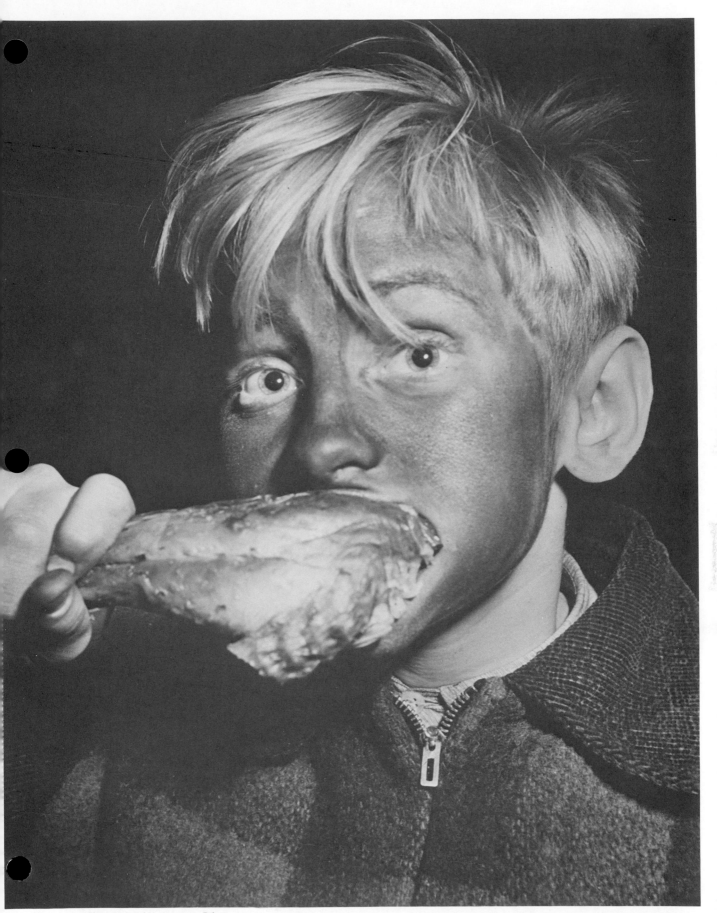

Photography of H. Armstrong Roberts

HANDBOOK

INTRODUCTION

A traveler in France can survive without knowing French, but the trip is likely to be easier and more pleasant for someone who knows the native tongue. In the same way, an American needs to know a particular dialect of American English called Standard Written English—SWE. We can survive without knowing it, but we'll be a lot better off if we have mastered it.

Standard Written English is not very different from any other dialect of American English. It uses much the same vocabulary and the same grammar as the others, but in addition it has certain conventions so widely accepted that everyone recognizes them as characteristic of SWE. That is what makes it "standard": it is essentially the same wherever it is used, whether in Maine or Alabama, whether by black person or by white, whether by plumber or by banker.

Because it is a standard which most people know and value, Standard Written English is probably more useful in a general way than any of our other dialects. For this reason, it is important for you to learn it. Although perhaps it should not be so, the best jobs and the greatest social prestige still fall to those who have mastered Standard Written English. Having mastered it does not guarantee, of course, that the user will always write effectively or that what that person writes will be beautiful or even sensible (the lowest thoughts and worst nonsense can be expressed in SWE), but at least everyone will be able to see the error or foolishness in what is written and thus be prepared to deal with it. Standard Written English aids in clarity of expression, not necessarily in quality of thought.

Well, what are the characteristics of this valuable standard dialect? Conventionality, mostly. Writers of Standard Written English are expected, for instance, to employ "correct"—that is, conventional—grammar and usage: verbs agree with subjects, pronouns appear in the proper cases, and so on. Furthermore, writers of Standard Written English must spell the words of English in a conventional way; "creative" spelling won't do. They must choose the appropriate words for any given writing situation, too, and not resort to their own special dialects or to slang. Finally, they must follow the accepted conventions in the matters of capitalization and punctuation. In a way, then, Standard Written English is the "correct" English of the schoolteacher and the blue-penciling editor.

As such, it might be pretty stiff and sterile, with all the juice of personality squeezed out. It need not be, though. In the hands of a competent writer, Standard Written English can soar and sing as well as any other dialect and probably better than most. Certainly it is the one likely to have the largest audience. Most writing in books and magazines, for instance, is in SWE.

Fortunately, Standard Written English can be learned fairly easily by those who know any other variety of English. (Presumably those learning English as a second language will have special, different problems not dealt with here.) The reason SWE is fairly easy for native English speakers to learn is simple: those who know English already know almost everything they will need to know about Standard Written English; therefore, they need only concentrate on its special conventions to add it to their present dialect.

At any rate, that is what this whole Handbook is about: the conventions of Standard Written English. If you can already speak, read, and write English, you can learn to produce Standard Written English by mastering the material in the Handbook. It is the sort of material that you have probably been exposed to many times before in school, so many times, indeed, that you may be thoroughly bored, frustrated, or both by it. If you are bored because you already know SWE, you can skip the Handbook; if you are frustrated because you have tried before to master Standard Written English and have not done so, remind yourself that it is both important and easy to learn. Consult the Handbook whenever you need to.

At any rate, don't give up. This time you *can* get it right, all of it, and you won't ever have to face the problem of studying it again. You'll have it, and you'll have the most useful dialect of all.

A note about the arrangement of the Handbook. Each of the forty items begins with a brief statement of the rule being introduced. This is followed by an expanded explanation of the rule and by exercises for practice. The brief statement may be all you need to remind you of what you already know, or the longer explanation may be necessary to provide information you do not know. Either you or your instructor will decide whether or not you need to do the exercises.

The Handbook includes information on grammar and usage, punctuation and capitalization, style, and spelling. In the back of the book is an index to help you find items in the Handbook.

Avoid sentence fragments—groups of words which are not really sentences at all but which are written as if they were complete sentences, with a capital at the beginning and a period at the end, like this:

With a match in his hand.

The boy running as fast as possible.

When the alligator slid into the water.

After direct questions, fragments are permissible:

Where is America headed? Straight toward disaster.

Why did he act that way? Because he was jealous.

Fragments are permissible when they are exclamations:

What a day!

Never again!

In Standard Written English, most sentences (a few exceptions will be discussed later) must be grammatically complete. That means that each sentence must have at least a simple subject and a verb, which work together to express an idea that can stand alone. Examples of a very simple sentence might be

Dogs bark.

Lions roar.

There aren't very many sentences quite that simple, however, and we would sound odd if we constantly used that kind of sentence. Most of us use more complicated sentences most of the time, so most of our sentences are made with a *subject* which may include more than just the simple subject (for example, "The clever girl" instead of just "The girl") and a *predicate* which includes the verb but may have other words in it, too. Look at these examples:

SIMPLE SUBJECT   VERB
Her most difficult trick   thrills every audience.

COMPLETE SUBJECT   COMPLETE PREDICATE
The thin old man   walks briskly through the park each day.

The subject is usually a noun, which is the name of something (dog, woman, building, chair, tree, love, hate, respect, etc.), or some substitute for a noun, like a pronoun (he, they, everyone, all), or a phrase (growing a garden, learning to ski, cutting the grass). Here are some examples:

131

SUBJ
The **dog** was running up the street as if his tail were on fire.

SUBJ
Love is the most desired emotion people have.

SUBJ
He demands all my time.

SUBJ
Everyone decided to go to the movies.

SUBJ
Learning to ski takes a great deal of time and energy.

SUBJ
Cutting the grass is a chore that practically nobody likes.

The verb is a word that tells what action is taking place in the sentence (runs, walks, cries, calls, loves, hits, etc.) or a word that shows that something exists (is, seems, appears, becomes). Verbs may appear in either a simple form (one word) or a compound form (two or more words) because verbs, besides showing what is happening in a sentence, show time (present, past, future). Here are some examples:

VERB
That child **cries** all the time! *(simple form)*

VERB
He **slept** hard all night. *(simple form)*

VERB
She **will go** to the hearing tomorrow. *(compound form)*

VERB
They **have gone** to that resort before. *(compound form)*

There are three kinds of sentences in English: the *declarative* sentence (the ordinary kind that we use most, that ends with a period); the *interrogative* sentence (just a fancy word for a question, like "Who forgot to lock the door?" or "Why are you leaving so early?"); and the *imperative* sentence, which is a command, like "Look out!" or "Please put the milk in the refrigerator." or "Get away from me!" Notice that all declarative sentences (the ordinary ones) and interrogative sentences (questions) must have a subject and a verb to be complete; but imperative sentences (commands) do not have a stated subject. Instead, their subject is always the word "you," which is understood but not written down. There is always a verb, and there may be other words involved, but there is no written subject.

There are two other kinds of sentences which do not require a written subject and verb to be complete: direct answers to questions, and exclamations. Here is an example of each:

132

What color is your car? **Red-brown.**

Hurray for Texas!

Sentences which do not meet the requirements set forth above are incomplete. They are called fragments and should not be used in Standard Written English. So check each of the ordinary sentences and the questions that you write to make sure that they have a subject and a verb, plus whatever other words help you say what you want to.

One kind of fragment which occurs very commonly and which you should be especially careful to avoid is the clause which begins with what we call a subordinating conjunction (although, while, when, where, after, unless, as if, and so on; see p. 254 for a complete list) or by a relative pronoun (who, whom, which, that) when these are not the first word in a question. Any unit with its own subject and predicate is called a clause, but not all clauses are independent—that is, not all clauses can be whole sentences by themselves. Clauses that are preceded by a subordinating conjunction or a relative pronoun are correct enough in themselves, but cannot stand alone as sentences, because the words at the beginning of these clauses indicate that something else is needed to complete the idea so that the sentence will make sense. Here are some examples of subordinate clauses used both incorrectly and correctly.

Before the nation can recover fully *(fragment)*

Because no one ever asked him *(fragment)*

These units may serve as parts of sentences, but not alone as whole ones.

Before the nation can recover fully, we must have a new economic plan. *(complete sentence)*

Because no one ever asked him, he did not reveal the secret. *(complete sentence)*

One other sort of fragment has no subordinating word and has both a subject and a verb, but it has the verb in the wrong form. Usually that is some -ing form without a helping verb. Sometimes the wrong form of the verb is the past participle of an irregular verb used without a helping verb. Here are examples of both incorrect and correct use of each of these forms:

A large black cat **strolling** slowly along the back fence *(fragment)*

A large black cat **was strolling** along the back fence. *(complete sentence)*

The necklace **stolen** from Cartier's *(fragment)*

The necklace **was stolen** from Cartier's. *(complete sentence)*

There are many sorts of fragments, of course. The best way to avoid all of them is to be sure that every sentence has a subject and a verb working together to make a statement and that the statement makes sense by itself and does not require additional words to be a complete idea.

Avoid fused sentences. Fused sentences occur when two or more sentences are run together with no punctuation between them, like this:

It was cold outside we soon decided to go into the shack.

I was sorry when Abe arrived he turned out to be a bully.

Wars are very expensive furthermore they do no good anyway nobody wins.

(Both fused sentences and comma-spliced sentences are sometimes called *run-on sentences.*)

A clause without a subordinating word in front of it can stand alone. Such a clause is called an independent clause. An independent clause can therefore be a sentence, and every sentence must have at least one independent clause. Some sentences, of course, have more than one clause.

We join independent clauses together to make more complicated sentences sometimes, by means of coordinating conjunctions (and, but, for, or, nor, yet) preceded by a comma.

CONJ
The pencil was defective, **and** I had no pen.

CONJ
His ski binding broke, **but** he was able to keep from falling down.

When two independent clauses are run together without a coordinating conjunction and without punctuation, the result is a fused sentence, a construction that should be avoided.

The hurricane began early in the morning it continued until mid-afternoon. *(fused sentence)*

The hurricane began early in the morning, and it continued until mid-afternoon. *(correct sentence)*

The most commonly used way to avoid fused sentences is to use a coordinating conjunction and a comma whenever you join two independent clauses, as shown above.

Another way to avoid fused sentences is to make separate sentences out of the two independent clauses.

The lines at the check-out counters were incredibly long Julio liked baseball better than shopping. *(fused sentence)*

The lines at the check-out counters were incredibly long. Julio liked baseball better than shopping. *(separate sentences)*

A third way to avoid fused sentences is to use a semicolon between independent clauses when the ideas in them are closely related.

She wanted to talk only with Jeremy no one else would do. *(fused sentence)*

She wanted to talk only with Jeremy; no one else would do. *(correct sentence)*

Avoid comma-spliced sentences. Comma-spliced sentences are two sentences run together with only a comma and no conjunction between them, like this:

Airplanes require high-octane fuel, this is hard to manufacture.

Anna arrived late, however I forgave her this time.

Milk contains calcium, everyone needs calcium in his or her diet.

(Both comma-spliced sentences and fused sentences are sometimes called *run-on sentences.*)

When two independent clauses are joined together by only a comma, with the coordinating conjunction left out, the result is a comma-spliced sentence, a construction that should be avoided.

The cat put up a terrible yowl, windows flew up all over the neighborhood. *(comma-spliced sentence)*

The cat put up a terrible yowl, and windows flew up all over the neighborhood. *(correct sentence)*

The best way to avoid comma-spliced sentences is to be sure that you use a coordinating conjunction along with the comma whenever you join two independent clauses.

You can also avoid comma-spliced sentences by making two separate sentences of the independent clauses or by using a semicolon instead of a comma between independent clauses. (See Rule 2.)

Be sure that your verbs agree with your subjects in number.

Singular subjects take singular verbs:

    SUBJ   VERB
A **guide dog** never **chases** cats.

    VERB SUBJ
There **is** a **hair** in my soup.

    SUBJ   VERB
That **orchestra plays** very well.

("Each," "either," and "neither" are always singular.)

Plural subjects take plural verbs:

    SUBJ   VERB
Girls these days often **wear** pants.

    SUBJ   VERB
Tom and Emily are leaving together.

In "or" sentences, the verb agrees with the closer subject:

Either the **dog** or the **cats keep** me awake all night.

As was noted earlier, all clauses have subjects and verbs. Most of the time what is known as agreement of subject and verb (singular subjects take singular verbs and plural subjects take plural verbs) gives no trouble. This is because in most tenses the verb has only one form. However, in the present tense the verb does change form in the third person singular. Therefore, in the present tense we must be sure that we choose the right verb to agree with the subject.

The pattern of a verb (except "to be," which is like no other verb) is therefore like this in the present tense:

I drive	we drive
you drive	you drive
he drives	they drive

Note that the verb adds -s in the third person singular. This is where the problem of agreement arises. Whenever the subject is singular and in the third person, use the -s form; whenever the subject is first or second person or third person plural, use the form without the -s.

Notice that in all other tenses except present tense there is only one form of the verb:

I walked	we walked
you walked	you walked
he walked	they walked

151

Agreement of subject and verb is obviously no problem here.

When the verb form contains "have" as a part of it, "have" changes to "has" in the third person singular.

She **has** driven her boyfriend to school all week.

The stock market **has** fallen steadily this month.

All nouns are third person, either singular or plural.

Collective nouns, those naming a group of people or things, are almost always considered singular. When collective nouns are the subjects of clauses, they take singular verbs. When they are antecedents of pronouns they take singular forms of the pronoun.

The **team is** certain to win this year. **It has** several veterans back from last year's championship team.

Plurals in regular nouns are made by the addition of -s or -es (see Rule 5 for a discussion of irregular nouns). Plural nouns take plural verbs, of course.

When singular nouns or pronouns are linked together by "and" into one subject, the subject becomes plural.

SUBJ CONJ   SUBJ   VERB
The **boy** and his **father** seldom **speak** to one another.

S   CONJ S   VERB
She and **I have** little in common.

SUBJ   SUBJ   CONJ   VERB
Mrs. Worthington, Mr. Archer, and **Ms. Porter have been called** to headquarters for a conference.

In the special construction with "either . . . or" and "neither . . . nor," the subject does not automatically become plural, as it does with "and." The verb agrees with the closer subject.

SUBJ   SUBJ   VERB
Either the **nails** or the **lumber continues** to arrive late.

SUBJ   SUBJ   VERB
Either the **lumber** or the **nails continue** to arrive late.

The way to avoid subject-verb agreement problems is to be sure to identify properly the subject and the verb, no matter how much material there may be in between and no matter what kind it is.

SUBJECT-VERB AGREEMENT

The **elephant**, stalked through the jungle by a brace of tigers, **continues** feeding, unaware of the danger. ("Continues" is singular, to agree with the singular subject, "elephant.")

Against the orders of their mother, the **children**, assisted by their dog, **ravage** the trash cans in the alley. ("Ravage" is plural to agree with the plural subject, "children.")

Furthermore, remember that the verb agrees with its subject, not with some other word in the sentence.

The **prize was** two tickets to the circus. (The subject of "was" is "prize," not "tickets.")

Pancakes were the main item on the menu. (The subject of "were" is "pancakes," not "item.")

One last word: not all words that end in -s are plurals—

The **news is** good.

Politics is a dirty business.—

but most of them are. And all nouns preceded by "each," "every," "either," or "neither" are singular, as are the pronouns "each," "either," and "neither"; all take singular verbs.

SUBJECT-VERB AGREEMENT

Most nouns form their plurals by the addition of -s or -es.

The **bees** were divided into two **classes**.

Some commonly used nouns, however, form their plurals in other ways. Be sure to memorize and use properly these irregular nouns.

Several **men** came into the room.

He marched as if he had two left **feet**.

Doris put the **children** to bed.

Some nouns ending in -f or -fe change to -ves in the plural:

wife, wives

wolf, wolves

loaf, loaves

If in doubt, consult a dictionary.

Use 's to form the plural of letters, numerals, and words used as words.

Although the vast majority of nouns in English form their plurals by the addition of -s or -es, some do not. Those that do not are in two classes. ("Children" and "oxen" as the plurals of "child" and "ox" make up a small third class.)

The first of these classes is the irregular nouns that have separate forms for the plural or use one form for both singular and plural. Though the number of such nouns is small, the nouns are fairly common ones.

bison	bison	moose	moose
deer	deer	mouse	mice
foot	feet	series	series
goose	geese	sheep	sheep
grouse	grouse	swine	swine
louse	lice	tooth	teeth
man	men	woman	women

The second class is made up of foreign-derived nouns, many from Latin. When they first came into the language, they kept the plurals from their language of origin, but by now many of them have also developed regular plurals in -s or -es. For instance, "memorandum" may have either "memoranda" or "memorandums" as the plural form. Here is a partial list of nouns that have retained irregular plurals. (Some also have regular plurals.)

alumna	alumnae	crisis	crises
alumnus	alumni	criterion	criteria

analysis	analyses	fungus	fungi (or funguses)
basis	bases	medium	media
beau	beaux (or beaus)	nucleus	nuclei
cactus	cacti (or cactuses)	syllabus	syllabi

Adding -s or -es can be a little more complex than it seems, for the basic spelling of the noun may change as it becomes plural. For instance, "body" becomes "bodies" in the plural, just as do most other nouns ending in "y" preceded by a consonant. For further information about spelling plurals, see the spelling rules in a dictionary.

With the following exceptions, *never* use an apostrophe to make nouns plural.

The plurals of letters, numerals, or words referred to as words are made by adding an apostrophe and an -s:

His **7's** were hard to read.

Don't make your **m's** look like **w's**.

He used fourteen **you know's** in his speech.

Remember that letters, numerals, and words referred to as words are the **only** cases in which an apostrophe is used to make a plural.

Except in irregular verbs (see Rule 7), the past tense and past participle of verbs are formed by adding -d or -ed. Be sure to add them even if they are not pronounced clearly or sound like -t:

He use**d** to go early in the day.

What am I suppose**d** to do now?

Ellsworth rack**ed** up the balls again.

She has often skat**ed** down the canal.

While Ferguson attack**ed** to the north, Griswold slipp**ed** down the Cold Creek Valley Road on the left flank.

Form the past tense of regular verbs by adding -d or -ed to the basic form: care/cared, look/looked. The failure in writing to add -d or -ed to verbs which need them is the result of our not always hearing the signals in speech. Because of the nature of our speech mechanisms and the nature of the sound system of our language, in speech we often run similar sounds together. For instance, the final sound of the word "proposed" gets blended with and partially if not completely lost in the next sound in the sentence, "I proposed to go alone."

However, we must not leave off the past tense signals when we write, for the written word has no sound. It must speak to us by its form, and if we leave off endings we have changed the form and therefore the meaning. When you need -d or -ed, put it on in your writing.

Most verbs form the past tense and past participle by the addition of -d or -ed. An important group of frequently used verbs, however, does not. Be sure to memorize and use properly the past tense and past participle of *irregular verbs*.

I **ran** down the street; I have **run** there many times.

He **drank** some water after he had **drunk** the bourbon.

She **went** to the same store she had **gone** to before.

> Do not confuse "sit" with "set," "rise" with "raise," or "lie" with "lay." "Lay" is a regular verb a little disguised (lay/laid/laid); the rest mentioned above are irregular.

As noted in Rule 6, the past tense of most verbs is made by adding -d or -ed. However, a fairly large number of verbs, called irregular verbs, do not follow this pattern. Instead, they have special forms for the past tense, the past participle, or both, or they have only one form for all three functions. Of the two hundred or so such verbs in the English language, the ones in the following list are perhaps the most frequently misused. If you do not know them, make it a point to learn them as soon as possible.

arise	arose	arisen	lie	lay	lain
begin	began	begun	lose	lost	lost
bend	bent	bent	ring	rang	rung
break	broke	broken	ride	rode	ridden
build	built	built	rise	rose	risen
burst	burst	burst	run	ran	run
choose	chose	chosen	see	saw	seen
come	came	come	set	set	set
cut	cut	cut	shake	shook	shaken
do	did	done	show	showed	shown
eat	ate	eaten	sink	sank	sunk
fly	flew	flown	sit	sat	sat
get	got	got (gotten)	speak	spoke	spoken
give	gave	given	swim	swam	swum

grow	grew	grown		take	took	taken
lay	laid	laid		throw	threw	thrown
lead	led	led		write	wrote	written

Be sure to use the second form for the past tense, the third form with the helping verbs "have," "has," and "had."

Yesterday he **wrote** a letter.

He **has written** a letter every day.

The verbs "lie" and "lay" pose a special problem, because the past tense form of "lie," an irregular verb, is spelled the same as the present tense form of "lay," a regular verb.

lie	**lay**	lain
lay	laid	laid

(The "lie" that means to tell an untruth is a different verb entirely, regular in form: lie, lied, lied.)

"Lie" is an intransitive verb meaning to recline; it does not take a direct object.

I **lie** in the sun whenever I can.

Yesterday I **lay** in the sun for two hours.

I have **lain** in the sun every day this week.

"Lay" is a transitive verb meaning to put or place; it does take a direct object.

Usually I **lay** my cards on the table.

Yesterday I **laid** them there.

I am sure I have **laid** them there each day this week.

"Sit" and "set" are another pair of verbs that are often confused. "Sit" is an intransitive verb meaning to get into a sitting position; it does not take a direct object. Notice that "sit" is very similar to "lie" and can be used in just the same ways.

I **sit** in the sun whenever I can.

Yesterday I **sat** in the sun for two hours.

I have **sat** in the sun every day this week.

"Set" is a transitive verb meaning to put or place, just like "lay"; it does take a direct object.

Usually I **set** my cards on the table.

Yesterday I **set** them there.

I am sure I have **set** them there each day this week.

Finally, "rise" and "raise" are another pair of confusing verbs. "Rise" is an intransitive verb meaning to go up by itself; it does not take a direct object.

The smoke **rises** straight up in the still air.

The balloon **rose** majestically into the sky.

The price of meat has **risen** sharply in the last week.

"Raise" is a transitive verb meaning to lift something up; it does take a direct object.

I **raise** the flag each morning at work.

The bumper jack **raised** the car eight inches.

I have **raised** my hand each time the teacher has asked for a volunteer.

Some of the verb forms in the following sentences are incorrect. Rewrite the sentences correctly in the space provided. If a sentence is correct, put a C in the space provided.

1. Yesterday I was so tired by early afternoon that I ~~laid~~ *lay* down and took a two-hour nap.

   Yesterday I was so tired by early afternoon that I lay down and took a two-hour nap

2. Have you drawn unemployment compensation this year?

   C

3. The best moment of the day is when I get home from work, ~~set~~ *sit* down in my chair, and take off my shoes.

   The best moment of the day is when I get home from work, sit down in my chair, and take off my shoes.

4. I *had* seen both the cow and the calf behind the barn.

   I had seen both the cow and the calf behind the barn.

5. Carlos ~~come~~ *came* running up the street as if his pants were on fire!

   Carlos came running up the street as if his pants were on fire

6. "Sit yourself down," said Grandpa.

   "Sit down," said Grandpa.

7. It seems as if I have ~~went~~ *gone* to the store twenty times this week.

It seems as if I have gone to the store twenty times this week.

8. He has ~~ran~~ *run* that machine for twenty years without an accident.

He has run that machine for twenty years without an accident.

9. The smoke ~~raised~~ *rose* slowly up from the fireplace and drifted off across the trees.

The smoke rose slowly up from the fireplace and drifted of across the trees.

10. Carefully she ~~lay~~ *laid* the delicate rose on the table.

Carefully she laid the delicate rose on the table.

Writing Practice

Write a paragraph about an important incident in your life, correctly using at least five of the verbs in the list in this section in the past tense. Do you dare to try "lie" and "lay"?

When I was a kid I had lain under the trees watching the animals feed on the green pasture. We depended on animals to cultivate our land so I have sat in the sun every day of the week to feed the animals. I always laid the food on the sled so it won't get wet. Our hen always laid eggs every day so we always had fresh eggs for breakfast.

With personal pronouns and the word "who," use the subjective form for subjects (SUBJ) and subject complements (SC), the objective form for direct objects (DO), indirect objects (IO), and objects of prepositions (OP), and the possessive form to show ownership (POSS).

SUBJ   IO POSS
I gave **him** **her** ball.

SUBJ SUBJ   DO   SC
The **one** **who** did **it** was **I**.

POSS   OP
Tom recovered **his** car from **them**.

Do not use "them" in any place where "those" would be appropriate:

He won't like them shoes. (*incorrect*)

He won't like those shoes. (*correct*)

Do not use "theirselves" for "themselves" or "hisself" for "himself." There are no such words as "theirselves" and "hisself" in Standard Written English.

In modern English, the personal pronouns and the relative pronoun "who" are the only words that retain the language feature called "case," the use of special forms of words to show grammatical relationships. Anglo-Saxon, the ancestor of English, had this feature in nouns as well as pronouns, and many languages still spoken today, like German, also have it. Fortunately for us, we have to worry about case in only two limited sets of words. Still, we do have trouble with case and must understand where to use which form. Here is a chart of the words in question:

PERSON	SUBJECTIVE		OBJECTIVE		POSSESSIVE	
	Singular	**Plural**	**Singular**	**Plural**	**Singular**	**Plural**
First	I	we	me	us	my, mine	our, ours
Second	you	you	you	you	your, yours	your, yours
Third	he	they	him	them	his	their, theirs
	she		her		her, hers	
	it		it		its	
	who	who	whom	whom	whose	whose

The subjective case is always used for the **subjects** of clauses:

SUBJ   SUBJ
Him and **me** went to the store. (*incorrect*)

SUBJ   SUBJ
He and **I** went to the store. (*correct*)

We came home again right away. *(correct)*

The subjective case is also used for *subjective complements*, words that come after certain verbs and refer to the subject. The verbs that can make sentences with subjective complements are few, but frequently used. The most important ones are "to be," "to become," "to seem," and "to appear." They are often called linking verbs. They link the subject and the subjective complement, which are in some way then indicated as the same:

Do you remember Anna? The ^{SUBJ} **girl** in the picture ^{VERB VERB SC} **appears to be she.**

^{SUBJ VERB SC}
It was they who brought the potato salad.

The ^{SUBJ} **one** in the back ^{VERB} **seems** to be ^{SC} **he.**

(The subjective case is sometimes called the nominative case and the subjective complement the predicate nominative.)

The objective case is used for the direct object of the verb, the indirect object of the verb, and the object of the preposition.

A direct object is a noun or pronoun coming after the verb and having a direct relationship with the verb. It is sometimes said to receive the action of the verb. Not all verbs can take direct objects, but many can. The direct object in any sentence names something different from the subject:

The ^{SUBJ} **monster greeted** ^{DO} **me** warmly.

^{SUBJ VERB DO}
Elise caught him in the pantry with the cook.

^{SUBJ VERB DO}
I pity them.

The sort of verb that can take a direct object is called a transitive verb. The sort that cannot but is not a linking verb either is called an intransitive verb. Many verbs are either transitive or intransitive, depending upon the sentences in which they occur.

The indirect object is a noun or pronoun that occurs only in sentences with a direct object, which it always precedes. It is the word showing to or for whom the action of the verb is directed. It occurs with only a rather limited number of verbs. There is an easy way to test a word to see if it is an indirect object. If you can put the word "to" or "for" in front of the word and the sentence still makes sense, that word is an indirect object. Try it with the examples given here. Although the sentences may sound a little awkward to you when you put in the "to" or "for," notice that they **do** make sense.

PRONOUN CASE

The **manager gave him** a **raise**.

My **uncle brought her** a new **coat**.

Harold showed me his **album**.

The object of a preposition is a noun or pronoun that occurs after a
preposition and works with it in making a prepositional phrase.

I noticed a mean streak **in them**.

George drove home **ahead of me**.

Prepositions may be more than one word. Here is a list of words and word
combinations often used as prepositions:

about	below	in front of	past
above	beneath	in place of	rather than
according to	beside	in regard to	regarding
across	between	in spite of	round
after	beyond	in view of	since
against	but (=except)	inside	through
ahead of	by	instead of	throughout
along	concerning	into	to, unto
among	contrary to	like	toward, towards
apart from	despite	near	under
around	down	of	underneath
as	during	off	until, till
as far as	except, excepting	on	up
at	for	on account of	up to
back of	from	out	upon
because of	in	out of	with
before	in addition to	outside	within
behind	in back of	over	without

In addition to their subjective and objective forms, the personal pronouns
also have possessive forms:

	Singular	Plural
First person:	my, **mine**	our, **ours**
Second person:	your, **yours**	your, **yours**

179

Third person:	his, **his**	their, **theirs**
	her, **hers**	
	its	

The possessive forms not in bold faced type above are used in front of nouns, as adjectives: my hat, your gloves, its tail, our car, your house, their daughter. The bold faced possessive forms ("his" is the same in both cases) are used after verbs or the preposition "of" and do not precede nouns:

That hat is **mine**.

The house on the corner is **theirs**.

Do you like that new dress of **hers**?

In none of the possessive forms of the personal pronoun do we use the apostrophe. Unlike nouns and some other pronouns, whose possessive forms always contain an apostrophe, possessive personal pronouns never take an apostrophe.

The most troublesome possessive personal pronoun is "its," because it is so easily confused with "it's," a contraction for "it is."

its = belonging to it

it's = it is

It is easy to tell, though, whether you should use "its" or "it's" in a sentence. Just mentally say "it is" wherever you want to use "its" or "it's." If it makes sense in the sentence to say "it is," put in the apostrophe; it if makes no sense to say "it is," do not put an apostrophe in "its."

180

In some of the following sentences, the pronoun case is incorrect or the possessive case of the pronoun incorrectly contains an apostrophe. Rewrite these sentences correctly. If a sentence is correct, put a C in the space provided.

1. The trouble with my brother and I is that we're lazy.

    C

2. The cops thought they knew whom was running down the street.

    The cops thought they knew who was running down the street.

3. Just between you and I, it might have been Judy we saw at the drive-in.

    Just between you and me, it might have been Judy we saw at the drive-in.

4. Him and me are going to the game together.

    He and I are going to the game together.

5. That mountain lion isn't your's, it's her's.

    The mountain lion isn't yours, it's hers.

6. I'm sure it was he whom we saw slinking away in the alley behind the theater.

    I'm sure it was him, who we saw slinking away in the alley behind the theater.

7. I hate both of them, John and her.

I hate both of them, John and she.

8. I am going to take Mike and she to the show tonight.

I am going to take Mike and her to the show tonight.

9. Craig didn't like our new zoo as well as he liked their's.

Craig didn't like our new zoo as well as he liked theirs.

10. Cleo and Jake were sure it was she and him that had been spreading all the untrue rumors about them.

Cleo and Jake were sure it was her and him that had been spreading all the untrue rumors about them.

Writing Practice

Write a paragraph about your favorite person. Include at least two examples of pronouns used in each of the three cases.

President Ferdinand Marcos is a courageous man, he initiated a drastic change in the Philippine Government. He is sincere in his actions and has gained popularity among the people. If it was not for him, crime would have been very discouraging for tourists to visit the Islands. His leadership is outstanding compared to the previous leaders of that country. My love for my country, he said, is encouragement enough for me to devote my whole life to the preservation of peace. My last objective, he said, is to uplift the welfare and pride of the common people. Until that is attained, my mind will not be in peace.

Many pronouns, including most of the personal pronouns, have no specific meaning except as they refer to nouns already used (antecedents). Be sure your pronouns agree in number with their antecedents (s—singular, p—plural).

The **girl** was tired, but **she** kept right on.

Eliza liked **pancakes** and ate **them** often.

Everyone was concerned about **his** or **her** money.

All in attendance felt **they** had learned something.

Many pronouns, especially the personal pronouns "he," "she," "it," and sometimes "we" and "they," have no meaning except as they refer to nouns or other pronouns already mentioned, words called **antecedents**. All pronouns which need antecedents must have the same number (singular or plural) as their antecedents.

The problem of pronoun agreement arises mostly with the possessive forms of the personal pronouns, especially "their." We often feel that "their" sounds correct when its antecedent is really singular. But with a singular antecedent, we should use "his," "her(s)," or "its."

Here are the possessive forms of the personal pronouns: my, your, his, her(s), its, our, your, their.

The antecedents that give the most trouble are the indefinite pronouns "everybody" and "everyone," which are singular in form but often imply the plural.

Everyone in the room left **their** seats. *(incorrect)*

Everyone in the room left **his** or **her** seat. *(correct)*

All in the room left **their** seats. *(correct)*

Each of the horses kicked **its** jockey. *(correct)*

We returned **our** tickets to the window. *(correct)*

Be sure to determine carefully whether the antecedent you are using is singular or plural, and then use the pronoun that is the same in number as the antecedent. If the gender (masculine or feminine) of the antecedent is clear, choose the proper form of the personal pronoun.

185

The **woman** brought **her** car in for servicing.

She had **her** son with **her**, and I gave the receipt to **him**.

When you are using a singular indefinite pronoun (each, anyone, everyone, somebody, someone) as an antecedent, and that antecedent could be either male or female, or both, it is important to indicate that it could be either in the later pronoun. Traditionally, we have used only the masculine form to indicate both male and female, like this:

Everybody knows **his** own house best.

Nowadays, however, we realize that it is important that we avoid sexism in our writing, even though the result might look somewhat awkward; so the sentence above should be written like this:

Everybody knows **his or her** own house best.

Perhaps some day there will be a singular personal pronoun in our language that means either male or female. Several have been suggested. In the meantime, we must continue to use "his or her" or "his and her."

Some of the following sentences contain errors in pronoun agreement. Rewrite the incorrect sentences correctly. If a sentence is correct, put a C in the space provided.

1. If anyone calls, tell them I'll be back at six o'clock.

    If anyone calls, tell him I'll be back at six o'clock.

2. Everybody needs goals if they are to be successful.

    Everybody needs goals if he is to be successful.

3. The city is proud of their garbage disposal trucks.

    The city is proud of its garbage disposal trucks.

4. Did anyone leave the dance early because they thought the band was lousy?

    Did anyone leave the dance early because he or she thought the band was lousy.

5. Neither of the girls got their certificate.

    Neither of the girls got her certificate.

6. Golf instructors never give a student a club and tell them to go out and hit a ball.

    Golf instructors never give a student a club and tell him to go out and hit a ball.

7. A person who is constantly worried about the loss of their job is not likely to do very good work.

A person who is constantly worried about the loss of his job is not likely to do any good work.

8. When a student gets out of high school, they are completely accustomed to strict rules.

When a student gets out of high school, he is completely accustomed to strict rules.

9. Everyone in favor of the motion please raise their hand.

Everyone in favor of the motion please raise his hand.

10. Each student must make sure to return all library books in order to get his or her grades for the semester.

_C_

Writing Practice

Write a paragraph of at least five sentences about your learning to drive a car or ride a bicycle. Use the following pronouns correctly at least once in your paragraph: he, her(s), its, him, she, they, their(s), them. Underline each pronoun you use in the paragraph. Show which word is the antecedent of each pronoun by putting an "A" above each antecedent. Make sure your pronouns are the same number (singular or plural) as their antecedents.

188

PRONOUN AGREEMENT: Number

_____
_____
_____
_____
_____
_____
_____
_____
_____
_____

Be sure that the personal pronouns "he," "she," "it," and "they" (in all case forms) refer clearly to one antecedent:

Gloria had always wanted to study mechanical engineering because **they** are always in demand. *(incorrect)*

Gloria had always wanted to study mechanical engineering because mechanical engineers are always in demand. *(correct)*

Howard told George **he** couldn't find **his** watch. *(incorrect)*

Howard told George, "I can't find my watch." *(correct)*

Or,

Howard told George, "I can't find your watch." *(correct)*

Since many pronouns have no meaning except as they refer back to their antecedents, it is important that such pronouns refer clearly to antecedents fairly close to them. Pronouns which need antecedents but don't have them are very confusing to a reader.

Once upon a time a prince rode up to a great castle, for he knew that he could find **them** there.

"Them"? The pronoun has no antecedent, and consequently the sentence does not make sense. Here are some other examples of sentences made nonsense by pronouns without antecedents.

Let's go down to the store to see if they have **one** there.

Dominick wanted to go to Stanford Medical because **they** always make good money.

Perhaps in the future city government will provide funds for **it**, but right now **they** can't get any.

Some people work very hard for long hours, **which** is against union principles.

Here are some examples of pronouns with ambiguous antecedents.

Florence wanted to go with Geraldine, but **she** was too tired. (Who was too tired—Florence or Geraldine?)

The father told his son that **he** could fix the tire himself. (Will the father or the son fix the tire?)

The contractor explained to the banker that **his** building needed some expensive repairs. (Whose building—the contractor's or the banker's?)

Be sure that pronouns have single, clear antecedents. If they don't, your sentences will be in a hopeless snarl.

Remember, too, that pronouns must agree with their antecedents in number (singular if the antecedent is singular, plural if the antecedent is plural). See Rule 9.

One other consideration: use "who" and "whom" to refer to persons, "that" to refer either to persons or anything else, and "which" to refer to anything except persons. Persons in groups are referred to with "that."

The girl **who** moved next door is lovely.

A clerk **that** short-changes a customer should be fired.

Look at the lion **that** just ate the missionary.

This sack of manure, **which** I bought at a nursery, would cost only half as much at one of the dairies in Norwalk.

Any mob **that** forms today will have a hard time moving through the streets.

PRONOUN REFERENCE

Some of the following sentences contain pronouns that are unclear about which antecedent they refer to. Rewrite these sentences, showing clearly the relationship between each pronoun and its antecedent. If a sentence is correct, put a C in the space provided.

1. We unpacked our clothes from the suitcases and took them up to the attic.

We unpacked our clothes from the suitcases and took it up to the attic

2. Sue was arguing with her mother, and she looked unhappy.

Sue was arguing with her mother, and her mother looked unhappy.

3. One of the scouts told the scoutmaster he hadn't found the trail.

One of the scouts told the scoutmaster, he hasn't found the trail.

4. When Ed and Jim went back, they found that his apartment had been robbed.

When Ed and Jim went back, they found that their apartment had been robbed.

5. My girlfriend and her twin sister act so much the same that sometimes I can't tell when she is trying to fool me.

My girlfriend and her twin sister act so much the same that sometimes I can't tell when they are trying to fool me.

6. Martha called Heidi, and Heidi said that her grades had gone down.

Martha called Heidi, and she said that her grades had gone down.

7. When he put the chemical in the water, it turned green.

   When he put the chemical in the water, the mixture turned green.

8. She had taken that dollar from her purse and she didn't know where she put it.

   She has taken that dollar from her purse and she does not know where she laid it.

9. He had found a fork and spoon, but it was dirty.

   He had found a fork and spoon, but they are dirty.

10. A man which does those things should be run out of town.

    A man who does those things should be run out of town.

Writing Practice

In the following paragraph, draw a line from each pronoun to its antecedent, if it has one. If a pronoun has no antecedent but needs one, circle the pronoun. If a pronoun has no antecedent but does not need one, underline it.

Jerry was well liked in school, probably because he was always pleasant to everyone. He dated Jill most of the time, but she wasn't the only one, which was nice. Everybody in school did the same sort of thing. They were not yet ready to settle down to one girl. That pleased them, too, for they didn't want permanent attachments either, anymore than they did. The arrangement was a healthy one, for it allowed practice in adapting to various people. They found that practice useful as they grew older. All in all, it was a joyful time.

When using a personal pronoun, do *not* shift from first or third person to the second person.

> I walked a lot in the sun that summer, and **you** really get a good tan that way. *(incorrect)*

> I walked a lot in the sun that summer, and **I** really got a good tan that way. *(correct)*

Or,

> I walked a lot in the sun that summer, and **one** really gets a good tan that way. *(correct)*

The unnecessary shift of person in the personal pronoun does not often take place within one sentence, but from one sentence to the next. The practice of shifting from one person to another (the shift is almost always from first or third person to second person: "you") is at best awkward and at worst confusing, as in the following paragraph.

> I got up very early and went to Huntington Beach to go surfing. You really feel good early in the morning before the sky smogs up. I paddled out beyond the break and waited for the big ones to start in. Then I caught one. I hit the crest and started across the curl. It was wild! The spray hits your face and you think that you can't possibly stay up but you do, and then finally you come to the beach and drop into the water, sort of glad that you can stop and do it again. I turned my board around and started out again. It was nice to know you had the whole day ahead of you.

The passage would be more effective if the pronoun were the same throughout—in this case "I" (with "me" and "my" in the appropriate places).

Some changes in pronoun are inevitable, of course. However, you should avoid unnecessary ones like those in the example. They confuse rather than clarify.

Some of the following sentences have unnecessary shifts of person in the personal pronoun, first or third to second. Rewrite these sentences, keeping the use of person in the personal pronoun consistent. If a sentence is correct, put a C in the space provided.

1. I wish I had learned to drive sooner because you have a lot of fun behind the wheel.

    I could

    I wish I have learned to drive sooner, because I could have a lot of fun behind the wheel.

2. She jogs a lot because you get really good exercise that way.

    She jogs a lot because she gets good exercise that way.

3. I go to the country club because it does a lot of good things for you.

    I go to the country club because it does a lot of good things for me.

4. You can't get ahead in life unless you make some compromises.

    C

5. The seniors have a test at the end of two years that covers all you have learned.

    The seniors had a test at the end of two years that covered all they have learned.

Writing Practice

Write a paragraph about a picnic or other kind of social event you have attended. Use at least three personal pronouns in your paragraph, making sure you are consistent with your use of person in those pronouns.

_____

_____

_____

_____

_____

_____

_____

_____

_____

_____

_____

_____

_____

_____

_____

_____

_____

_____

_____

_____

_____

Do not confuse adverbs and adjectives in your writing.

> You did **good**. *(incorrect)*
>
> You did **well**. *(correct)*
>
> Martin will always be **bad**. *(adjective)*
>
> Martin will always perform **badly**. *(adverb)*

Adjectives modify (limit or describe) nouns; adverbs modify adjectives, verbs, or other adverbs. They are not interchangeable with each other. It is therefore necessary to learn which words are adjectives and which are adverbs.

Many adverbs end in -ly—cheerfully, wholly—but not all of them do—rather, very. Some adjectives end in -ly—homely, friendly—though most do not—sticky, truthful. (The -ly words made from adjectives—doubtful, doubtfully—are usually adverbs; those made from nouns—friendly, manly, a very few others—are adjectives.) A very large number of adverbs are -ly forms of adjectives, and they give us little trouble. Here are a few examples:

Adjective	Adverb	Adjective	Adverb
bad	badly	new	newly
bright	brightly	rare	rarely
close	closely	rough	roughly
loose	loosely	smooth	smoothly
loud	loudly	tight	tightly

Adverbs which do not end in -ly are sometimes confused with adjectives. "Good," an adjective, is often used where the adverb "well" is called for.

Charles performed the piano concerto **good.** *(incorrect)*

Charles performed the piano concerto **well.** *(correct)*

After linking verbs (see Rule 8) the adjective is proper. Some linking verbs not mentioned in Rule 8 are sensory verbs such as "feel," "taste," "look," "sound," and "smell." After these verbs, adjectives are also proper.

The old man **became cheerful**.

Charles Darwin **was careful** in his observations.

The situation **looks bad**.

Garbage **smells strong**.

After other verbs, adverbs are proper.

The old man **laughed cheerfully**.

Charles Darwin **observed carefully**.

The situation developed **badly**.

Garbage burns **slowly**.

The best way to determine whether a word in doubt is an adjective or an adverb is to consult a dictionary. At any rate, the two kinds of words should not be confused with one another.

ADJECTIVE-ADVERB CONFUSION

In some of the following sentences adjectives have been used where
adverbs should have been used or vice versa. Rewrite these sentences
correctly. If a sentence is correct, put a C in the space provided.

1. I feel badly about Doug's accident.

    _____

    _____

2. You look well in that dress.

    You look better in that dress

    _____

3. That stew smells marvelous!

    _____

    _____

4. Avocados taste horribly to me.

    Avocados taste horrible to me.

    _____

5. Her wig was so loose it slid into her soup.

    C

    _____

6. The movie was made really good. *well.*

    _____

    _____

201

7. Diane sang so bad at the party she'll never be asked to sing again.

   Diane sang so badly at the party, she'll never be asked to sing again.

8. Ella's corsage was beautiful and smelled very fragrantly.

   Ella's corsage was beautiful and smelled very fragrant.

9. What good is a comfortable car that doesn't run good?

   What good is a comfortable car that doesn't run well.

10. I ran quick so that I would not get caught.

    I ran quickly, so that I would not get caught

Writing Practice

Write a paragraph describing something you like to do on weekends. In your paragraph correctly use at least four adjectives and four adverbs. Then underline each adjective and circle each adverb. Finally, draw an arrow from each adjective and adverb to the word it modifies (limits or describes).

_____

_____

_____

_____

_____

_____

_____

_____

_____

_____

_____

_____

_____

_____

_____

_____

_____

_____

Do not write dangling modifiers.

> Reading the comics, a rooster pecked Myra's toes. (*incorrect*)
>
> Reading the comics, Myra felt a rooster peck her toes. (*correct*)

Dangling modifiers are usually participial phrases, structures made of the present or past participle of a verb (wish**ing** or wish**ed**) and an object or another phrase.

> **Watching the ball**, Jay tripped over the bat.
>
> The owl **trapped in the net** made pitiful little hooting sounds.

Participial phrases are adjectives that modify nouns. They need to be close to the nouns or pronouns they modify. If they are not, they are said to "dangle." Most often dangling participial phrases occur at the beginnings of sentences—but not always (see the second example above). They dangle when there is nothing for them to modify or when the words they are supposed to modify are too far away from them.

> **Dancing in the garden**, the blossoms tickled them. (nothing to modify)
>
> **Wagging his tail furiously**, I stroked the thick fur of the big Labrador. (modifier too far from word modified)
>
> **Caught in the police raid**, the sheriff carted both boys off to jail. (word modified unclear)

Whenever possible, be sure that the noun or pronoun modified is the first one after an introductory participial phrase.

Dancing in the garden, they were tickled by the blossoms.

Wagging his tail furiously, the big Labrador let me stroke his thick fur.

Caught in the police raid, the boys were carted off to jail by the sheriff.

Other modifiers besides participial phrases can dangle or be misplaced, of course. See Rule 14 for these.

Some of the following sentences contain dangling modifiers. Rewrite these sentences correctly. If a sentence is correct, put a C in the space provided.

1. After considering the idea for a month, it was rejected by the belly dancers.

    After considering the idea for a month, the belly dancers rejected it.

2. To get promoted, good work on the job is needed.

    To get promoted on the job, good work is needed.

3. In crossing a busy street, ^you must great caution is necessary!

    Great caution is necessary in crossing a busy street.

4. Trapped by the heavy doors, terror showed on the faces of the boys as the fire swept down on them.

    Terror showed on the faces of the boys, trapped by the heavy doors, as the fire swept down on them.

5. When making ice cream, a freezer helps.

    A freezer helps, when making ice cream.

6. Hiding in the back bedroom, Juan heard his parents calling for him throughout   C
    the house.

    Juan, hiding in the back bedroom, heard his parents calling for him throughout the house

7. To be prepared for an extensive backpacking trip, training and know-how are essential.

   To be prepared, training and know-how are essential for an extensive backpacking trip.

8. While driving along a country road, a tortoise and a hare stepped in front of my car.

   A tortoise and a hare stepped in front of my car while I was driving along a country road.

9. Coming home from work today, the neighbor's canary attacked me.

   Coming home from work today, I was attacked by the neighbor's canary.

10. Being very deaf, rock and roll music doesn't bother my grandfather.

   My grandfather, being very deaf, isn't bothered by rock and roll music.

Writing Practice

Write a paragraph comparing two friends or relatives. In your paragraph, use at least three participial phrases correctly.

_____

_____

_____

_____

_____

_____

_____

_____

DANGLING MODIFIERS

_____

_____

_____

_____

_____

_____

_____

_____

_____

_____

_____

_____

Be sure that all modifiers are near the words they modify.

Alma used to enjoy swimming with her brother **at the age of ten**. *(incorrect)*

At the age of ten, Alma used to enjoy swimming with her brother. *(correct)*

Only I washed the van. *(Nobody helped me.)*

I washed **only** the van. *(I didn't wash the Honda.)*

I **only** washed the van. *(I didn't wax it.)*

I washed the **only** van. *(There was just one.)*

In addition to participial phrases (Rule 13), any word, phrase, or clause that qualifies or restricts the meaning of another word, phrase or clause is a modifier. A modifier is misplaced when it appears so far from what it is supposed to modify that the connection is no longer clear or the modifier seems to modify something else.

Trish adored anyone who helped her with her homework **with good justification**. *(incorrect)*

The modified word here is "adored," and the modifier should be closer to it.

With good justification, Trish adored anyone who helped her with her homework. *(correct)*

Or,

Trish adored, **with good justification**, anyone who helped her with her homework. *(correct)*

The way to solve the problem of misplaced modifiers is to change the order of the elements in a sentence until all the modifying relationships are clear. Usually, this means putting the modifier close to what it is supposed to modify; orphan modifiers wandering about in search of parents can ruin a sentence.

Some of the following sentences contain misplaced modifiers. Rewrite these sentences correctly, placing each modifier close to the word it modifies. If a sentence is correct, put a C in the space provided.

1. Margie got some pills from a specialist that made her feel better.

   Margie got some pills, that made her feel better from the a specialist.

2. Our sociology professor is always describing his journeys through Africa in our Sociology I class.

   Our sociology professor, in our sociologe I class, is always describing his journeys to Africa.

3. I'll proofread your paper when you finish for errors.

   I'll proofread your paper for errors, when you finish.

4. When looking at clouds, people should keep their feet firmly on the ground.   *C*

   People, when looking at clouds, should keep their feet firmly on the ground.

5. My mother bought one of those new kitchen gadgets from a fast-talking salesman that was guaranteed to peel potatoes in half the time.

   My mother bought one of those new kitchen gadgets, that was guaranteed to peel potatoes in half the time, from a fast-talking salesman.

213

Writing Practice

Write a paragraph directing a stranger to the nearest bank. In your paragraph, use any three of the following modifiers correctly: when counting the blocks, to get to the correct street, before making a right-hand turn, after passing the hospital, at the second traffic light, approaching the alley.

Do not use double negatives.

Bradley **didn't** want **no** trouble. *(incorrect)*

Bradley **didn't** want any trouble. *(correct)*

Or,

Bradley wanted **no** trouble. *(correct)*

Adriana could **not barely** lift the twenty-pound weight. *(incorrect)*

Adriana could **barely** lift the twenty-pound weight. *(correct)*

Although Chaucer, Shakespeare, and other distinguished authors of the past often used more than one negative to add emphasis (when they said no they really meant it), recent practice forbids using more than one negative, no matter how emphatic we want to be. The following words are considered negatives: no, none, not, nothing, never, barely, hardly, scarcely.

No man can allow that.

He has **never** flown a plane.

Harold could **hardly** do any better.

Once in a while we do construct sentences in which we want to negate a negation—"I did not exactly not want to go to the party, but I did not feel exactly excited about going, either"—but in no other circumstances should we use two negatives for the same negation.

Some of the following sentences contain double negatives. Rewrite these sentences correctly, using only one negative to express the idea. If a sentence is correct, put a C in the space provided.

1. She hasn't no reason to doubt your word.

    She has no reason to doubt your word.

2. My folks never had no trouble with my sister.

    My folks had no trouble with my sister.

3. They haven't hardly flown.

    They haven't flown.

4. Try again if you don't succeed the first time. *C*

    Try if you don't succeed the first time.

5. I didn't get nothing done today.

    I get nothing done today.

6. I didn't barely have a second left to myself.

    I didn't have a second left to myself.

7. I hadn't scarcely finished dinner when my girl friend walked in.

   I scarcely finished dinner when my girl friend walked in.

8. Although she said she liked me, she didn't ever call back.

   Although she said she liked me, she did not call back.

9. I won't have none of that soup.

   I won't have that soup.

10. Tom hasn't no business playing first; he's better in the field.

    Tom has no business playing first; he's better in the field.

Writing Practice

Write a paragraph in which you take a stand on some controversial issue (for example, capital punishment or legalized abortion). Correctly use the following negative words in your paragraph: hardly, never, scarcely, no, not. Do not use double negatives!

Capital punishment hardly discourage hardened criminals. If I am to decide I'll never remove capital punishment. Scarcely are criminals caught red handed. No criminal will ever admit a crime. Not one of them will say I did it.

Use "a" before words beginning with consonant sounds, like this:

> a blob, a crate, a dummy, a fish, a guest, a history book, a union

Use "an" before words beginning with vowel sounds, like this:

> an ax, an event, an hour, an issue, an ox, an understudy

Be sure to go by the sound, not the spelling.

Both "a" and "an," called articles, are singular markers of nouns. When you see an "a" or an "an" you know that a noun won't be far ahead. They are really two spellings of the same word. "A" is used when the word following it (not necessarily the next noun but the next word) begins with a consonant sound: *a* consonant, *a* big apple, *a* bushel of grain. "An" is used when the word following it begins with a vowel sound: *an* apple, *an* egg, *an* ocean of tears, *an* honest man.

The *sound* of the word following, not its spelling, is what counts. If in doubt, say the word, then choose the right form of the article to use with it: *a* eucalyptus tree, *an* honor.

"The," the other article, is either singular or plural and has only one form. You needn't worry about how the next word sounds when you write "the."

Some of the following sentences have an "a" where there should be an "an," or vice versa. Rewrite these sentences correctly in the space provided. If a sentence is correct, put a C in the space provided.

1. The cartoon shows a group of Cub Scouts walking toward a ice cream truck.

   The cartoon shows a group of Cub Scouts walking toward an ice cream truck.

2. I feel I could have earned a "A" in the course.

   I feel I could have earned an "A" in the course.

3. In the background one can see an ancient boat sailing in the open harbor.

   C

4. During the summer the evenings are very warm with an onshore breeze.

   C

5. If you have a early class it is fine, but if you have a ten o'clock class it is practically impossible to find a place to park.

   If you have an early class it is fine, but if you have a ten o'clock class it is practically impossible to find a place to park.

Writing Practice

Write a paragraph comparing two vegetables. Use each of the following words preceded by either "a" or "an," whichever is appropriate: yellow, salty, round, odor, acid, eupepsia.

A yellow fruit is ripe and sweet while a salty taste means the fruit is pickled.

A round eggplant tastes better than a long
one. Flowers with an odor like that must not
be good in perfume making. Juice from
grapefruit has an acid taste.

Do not use "of" for "have" or for " 've" (meaning "have"):

I could **of** gone to Timbuktu. *(incorrect)*

I could **have** gone to Timbuktu. *(correct)*

Or,

I could've gone to Timbuktu. *(correct)*

Do not use "of" with "had":

I could have gone to Timbuktu if I had **of** wanted to. *(incorrect)*

I could have gone to Timbuktu if I had wanted to. *(correct)*

Often when we speak we run our words together and otherwise take shortcuts: "Jeacherazuns?" may be the way we really say, "Did you eat your raisins?" However, we cannot use that kind of shortcut when we write. One of the frequent contractions in English, " 've" for "have," in such phrases as "I would've gone with you," might lead us to believe that the " 've" sound should be spelled like another word that sounds almost the same, "of." But "of" is an entirely different word and has nothing to do with the word "have," of which " 've" is the contraction. Do not, therefore, confuse "of" with " 've," and be careful to use each where it is appropriate.

Never use "of" with the word "had."

The bear would have killed the pig if the dog had not **of** been there. *(incorrect)*

The bear would have killed the pig if the dog had not been there. *(correct)*

Some of the following sentences use "of" where "have" or " 've" should be used, or use "of" with "had." Rewrite these sentences correctly. If a sentence is correct, put a C in the space provided.

1. You should of warned me that the steps were slippery.

_____

_____

2. I wish I hadn't of been the black sheep of my family.

_____

_____

3. If you had known about the party, would you of come?

_____

_____

4. They would of come to the swap meet, but they thought it was cancelled.

_____

_____

5. You shouldn't have jumped off the deep end.

_____ C _____

_____

Writing Practice

Write a creative excuse to your teacher explaining why you didn't do your homework. Use contractions of "have" (such as "would've") correctly at least five times and the preposition "of" correctly at least three times.

_____

_____

227

Use a period at the end of a sentence that makes a statement or gives a mild command and at the end of an indirect question:

Punctuation is a simple matter.

Get me the *TV Guide*.

Alonzo asked when you would be home.

Use a question mark at the end of a direct question:

What really happened to Judge Crater?

Use an exclamation point at the end of an exclamation:

Look out!

Use periods at the end of sentences that make a statement, give a mild command, or ask an indirect question.

Periods are one kind of end punctuation.

Stop at the market on your way home and get some hamburger.

Sheila wondered when he was going to call.

Use question marks at the end of direct (not indirect) questions.

Who boiled the rhubarb? *(direct question)*

He asked who boiled the rhubarb. *(indirect question)*

Use exclamation points after words, phrases, or sentences that give sharp commands or require heavy emphasis.

Fire!

How wonderful!

You look absolutely sensational!

These three kinds of end punctuation give us very little trouble except when they are used with quotation marks. Some simple rules apply here.
Periods always go inside quotation marks.

Fred said, "I promise I'll call you tonight."

Emily Dickinson wrote "I Heard a Fly Buzz When I Died."

David claimed that the assignment was "icky."

Question marks go inside quotation marks if the quoted material is a question.

Paula sobbed, "Why didn't they tell me?"

They go outside if the material outside of the quotation marks is a question.

When did Patrick Henry say, "Give me liberty or give me death"?

Question marks go inside if the material both inside and outside the quotation marks is a question (a rare situation).

Did John Denver write "Do You Know the Way to San Jose?"

The same rules that apply to question marks used with quotation marks apply to exclamation points. But don't use exclamation points very often, and never use more than one at a time.

END PUNCTUATION

Put the correct mark of end punctuation at the ends of the following
sentences. Be sure to be careful about where the punctuation mark goes if
there are quotation marks.

1.   Joe asked, "When is the paper due, Mr. Dimwitty?"

2.   When did Winston Churchill make his famous statement, "Never in the field of
     human conflict was so much owed by so many to so few"?

3.   She said, "I won't be in till very late tonight, Mother, so don't wait up for me."

4.   The teacher asked the students if they had done all the outside reading

5.   The driver persisted in honking his horn even though the car in front of him
     was obviously stalled

6.   Her brother hit her, and the little girl yelled, "Cut that out!"

7.   "We want a home run!" the crowd screamed.

8.   I wonder how important this animal once was.

9.   Who is he, and what is happening in this cartoon?

10. People succeed at being happy in the same way they succeed in loving, by
     building a liking for themselves for true reasons

Writing Practice

Write a passage of at least eight sentences on your favorite kind of weather.
Use all three end punctuation marks at least twice each. Include three direct
quotations.

_____

_____

_____

Use a comma before the conjunction in a compound sentence.

McNamara led the footmen up the east slope, and MacDougal was supposed to flank the east cliff.

The economy in general improved, but the construction business remained sluggish.

You may take seats in the rear, or perhaps you would prefer side seats nearer the front.

When two independent clauses are joined by a coordinating conjunction (and, but, or, nor, for, yet), a comma precedes the conjunction (see rules 2 and 3).

Marvin drove the big stagecoach, and Pete rode shotgun for most of the trip.

He could shout louder than anyone I know, but he couldn't sing worth a darn.

If the two clauses are very short and closely related, the comma may be omitted.

Marvin drove and Pete rode shotgun.

He could shout but he couldn't sing.

With the conjunction "for," always use the comma.

Ned fell asleep, for he was very tired.

If you are in doubt about using the comma with coordinate independent clauses, use it.

Some of the following sentences are incorrect. Rewrite these sentences, inserting a comma before the coordinating conjunctions. If a sentence is correct, put a C in the space provided.

1. The sentimental goodbyes are completed and the lovers go their separate ways.

   _____

   _____

2. The workers were also squeezing the olives with some sort of press and the oil from these olives was draining into a large jar.

   _____

   _____

3. It will not be difficult to get a job for auto mechanics are in great demand all the time.

   _____

   _____

4. The ring leader then called a halt, and we gathered around to eat the refreshments.

   _____

   _____

5. In lecture classes you are part of a group but that group can function very efficiently without you.

   _____

   _____

6. Everyone agreed that he seemed to be an incompetent dentist but none of them ever dreamed that he had a mouth full of cavities!

   _____

   _____

7. I have inquired about employment for you, and your experience will make it easy for you to find a job.

_____

_____

8. She will look for a new apartment or she will be asked to leave the one she is in now.

_____

_____

9. Ms. Washington urged all her students to take an active part in local government for she herself belonged to several committees concerned with civic affairs.

_____

_____

10. The campus and buildings are brand new yet the students complain about the facilities of the college.

_____

_____

Writing Practice

Write a paragraph explaining how to do something (boil an egg, get on a horse, make a paper airplane, etc.). Include at least five sentences that contain independent clauses joined by coordinating conjunctions.

_____

_____

_____

_____

_____

_____

_____

_____

_____

_____

_____

_____

_____

_____

_____

_____

_____

_____

_____

Use commas between all items in a series:

> Jackie likes raw clams, steamed clams, and fried clams.
>
> The pirate stole the gold, kissed the woman, and abandoned the ship.
>
> I can tell him, you can tell him, or we both can tell him.

A series, by definition, must include at least three items; it can include as many more as you happen to be talking about. Any list of items expressed in the same grammatical form can make a series: words, phrases, or clauses.

> **Honey**, **jam**, **syrup**, and **sugar** disappeared from the shelves very rapidly.
>
> The fox ran **over the rocks**, **through the creek**, **along the top of a stone fence**, and **into a narrow culvert**.
>
> **Ellery drove**, **I sang and told stories to keep him awake**, and **Oscar slept**.

All items in a series should be parallel; that is, each should be in the same grammatical construction. (See Rule 40 for more information on parallelism.)

> I liked the sun, being in the shade, and how the shadows looked. *(incorrect)*
>
> I liked the sun, the protection of the shade, and the look of the shadows. *(correct)*

Although practice on the matter varies, it is still preferable to use the comma between the next-to-last and last items in a series, as shown in all the examples here. The coordinating conjunction "and" or "or" as well as a comma precedes the last item.

Some of the following sentences need commas inserted between items in a series. Rewrite these sentences, putting the commas in the correct places. If a sentence is correct, put a C in the space provided.

1. During that week's vacation in California, we went skin-diving in the ocean, skiing in the mountains, and prospecting in the desert.

   _____

   _____

2. Hang-gliding flying and sky-diving are three of my favorite things to do.

   _____

   _____

3. Pat fixed me a huge breakfast: ham and eggs fruit juice toast and jam hot cakes potatoes and coffee.

   _____

   _____

4. Jack bought a new car, loaded it up with all his things, drove all night, and arrived at his new job at 8 a.m. the next day.

   _____

   _____

5. I found my way to the arena bought a ticket, and waited.

   _____

   _____

6. There are girls, boys, adults, and even a few pets.

   _____

   _____

7. You could get married get divorced, and have a baby in the same building if necessary.

_____

_____

8. We went through all the available houses in the areas that had good schools, recreational facilities safe streets, and access to the ocean.

_____

_____

9. You can go anywhere you want between classes and talk with friends eat lunch or do homework.

_____

_____

10. Some of the instruments used in the band were woodwinds drums, and chimes.

_____

_____

Writing Practice

Write a paragraph of at least six sentences on the kinds of entertainment available in your city or town. In your paragraph include at least two series, properly punctuated. Underline the sentences in which series appear.

_____

_____

_____

_____

_____

_____

Use commas to set off nonrestrictive elements in a sentence:

> The leading runner, who had on bright red shorts, fell at the water jump.
>
> The desk, which was a dark mahogany color, was not at all the kind he wanted.
>
> The new champion, a Finn, refused the medal.
>
> Our mail carrier, a girl with long hair and longer legs, is never late delivering our mail.

Since the use of commas with nonrestrictive elements depends upon identification of such elements, a definition is clearly in order. **Restrictive** modifiers are those necessary to limit the meaning of the word modified; the sentence would mean something different if the restrictive modifier was taken out. **Nonrestrictive** elements add further information but are not necessary for the completion of the meaning of the unit of which they are a part.

> Everyone **who threw a rock through a window** was arrested. *(restrictive)*
>
> The principal of Lowell School, **who drives a Pinto**, seldom has a parking problem. *(nonrestrictive)*

In the first example above, "Everyone was arrested" by itself would not mean the same thing as "Everyone who threw a rock through a window was arrested"; "who threw a rock through a window" is an essential modifier identifying what part of "everyone" was arrested. It is necessary to the meaning of the sentence and therefore grammatically restrictive, so it takes no commas. In the second example, "The principal of Lowell School seldom has a parking problem" is a sufficiently complete statement in itself; the information in "who drives a Pinto" is incidental, so commas are needed. Notice that you *could* put this information in a different sentence.

> The principal of Lowell School seldom has a parking problem. He drives a Pinto.

The consideration of restriction and nonrestriction arises most often with adjective clauses. Adjective clauses (as well as adverbial clauses; see Rule 22) are dependent clauses—that is, they cannot stand alone as sentences (see rules 1 and 2). For example, "who drives a Pinto" and "who threw a rock through a window" are not sentences by themselves; they must be a part of or attached to some independent clause. Because they have their own subject and predicate, such elements are clauses; because they begin with a relative, they are not independent. The relatives are the relative pronouns "who ("whom" in the objective case, "whose" in the possessive case), "that," and "which" and the relative adverbs "where" and "when."

The man **whom my sister married** is an avid fisherman. *(restrictive)*

The Queen of England, **who has little power today**, maintains the look of power through ritual. *(nonrestrictive)*

Tom Brown, **whose mother came from Ireland**, has vowed to visit Dublin within two years. *(nonrestrictive)*

A word **that strikes me as especially appropriate in this case** is "balderdash." *(restrictive)*

Milk, **which is high in butter fat**, brought premium prices in the days before margarine. *(nonrestrictive)*

Christmas is a time **when all rejoice.** *(restrictive)*

Each of the adjective clauses above modifies a noun, of course: man, Queen of England, Tom Brown, word, milk, time. Some of the clauses are restrictive, some nonrestrictive. The relative pronoun "that" almost always appears in a restrictive clause, the relative pronoun "which" almost always in a nonrestrictive.
The relative pronoun may be the subject of its clause.

The man **who came to dinner** stayed all night.
         SUBJ VERB

Or it may be the object of the verb in its clause.

The man **whom we fed** stayed all night.
         DO SUBJ VERB

Mr. Hunter's big white bitch, **which my children dearly loved**, had eight pups.
         DO   SUBJ   VERB

"Whom" and "which" in the two sentences above are the objects of verbs; they come first in their clauses instead of in the normal position of an object after the verb because they are also serving the function of connectors, relating the dependent clause to the independent clause.
As the examples above demonstrate, "who" is the subjective form of the relative pronoun, "whom" the objective form. No matter what the antecedent,

the relative pronoun takes the form—"who" or "whom"—appropriate to its function in its own clause.

Relative pronouns in the objective case may be left out in restrictive clauses but not in nonrestrictive clauses.

The man (whom) my sister married is an avid fisherman. *(restrictive)*

The dog (that) we used to have ran away. *(restrictive)*

Fido, whom the neighbors hated, unfortunately never ran away. *(non-restrictive)*

Once you understand the principle of restrictive and nonrestrictive elements, their punctuation ceases to be a problem: use commas to set off nonrestrictive elements; do not use commas with restrictive elements.

Most interrupting phrases within a clause are nonrestrictive and should be so punctuated. One special kind of element that is usually nonrestrictive is the *appositive*. An appositive renames an already stated noun.

The capital of Montana, **Helena**, sits in the mountains.

John Jones, the **letter carrier** in our neighborhood, will retire in a month.

I especially like jade, a green semiprecious **gem stone**.

All this may be more than you wanted to know about commas with nonrestrictive elements; but once you understand this principle, you won't often go wrong in your punctuation of sentences, for nonrestrictive elements present more problems in punctuation than anything else.

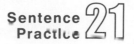

COMMA: Nonrestrictive Elements

Each of the sentences below has in it either a restrictive or a nonrestrictive clause. There are no commas in any of the sentences. Identify the nonrestrictive clauses and rewrite these sentences correctly. Put a C in the space provided for the sentences which contain restrictive clauses, since no commas are used with restrictive elements.

1. Miss Davis, my English teacher, recommended me for a scholarship.

    _____

    _____

2. The last book I read was not very interesting.

    _____ o/c _____

    _____

3. The girl who broke her leg was not hurt otherwise.

    _____ o/c _____

    _____

4. The debate team, which hasn't lost a meet, will appear here next week.

    _____

    _____

5. He introduced me to the club president, who came into the room just then.

    _____

    _____

6. The gun that was found did not belong to her friend.

    _____

    _____

7. Their new stereo, which Mr. Johnson bought in New York, has been giving them trouble ever since they've had it.

_____

_____

8. The car that was sold turned out to be a lemon.

_____ ok _____

_____

9. The box that she dropped contained nothing breakable.

_____ ok _____

_____

10. My sister Ellen, who is two years older than I, is coming home tomorrow.

_____

_____

Writing Practice

Write a paragraph describing any one building in your neighborhood. Put in your paragraph at least five correctly punctuated nonrestrictive elements, including examples of both adjective clauses and appositives.

_____

_____

_____

_____

_____

_____

_____

_____

COMMA: Nonrestrictive Elements

_____

_____

_____

_____

_____

_____

_____

_____

_____

_____

Use commas to set off introductory elements in a sentence:

Whenever Jonathan got the chance, he took all of Abigail's gumdrops.

In spite of this inexcusable behavior, Abigail loved Jonathan dearly.

As for me, I prefer jelly beans to gumdrops.

Usually introductory elements which are not part of an independent clause are set off from the rest of the sentence by a comma (especially if they are relatively long). The most common introductory elements are prepositional phrases, participial phrases, and adverbial clauses.

Prepositional phrases contain at least a preposition and an object of the preposition (see Rule 8). When they precede a clause, they are usually set off by a comma.

In the first place, I don't like oysters.

From the point of view of honesty, Bo is the best possible choice.

Instead of wearing her long dress, Jean chose jeans and a tee shirt.

Short prepositional phrases need not be set off:

In winter he froze; **in summer** he roasted.

At dusk I ran along the beach.

Participial phrases (see Rule 13) used as introductory elements are almost always set off with commas.

Holding the bat in his hand, Oliver Forney strode confidently to the plate.

Held back by his brother, Tom could only curse the man beating the horse.

Participial phrases preceded by "while," "when," and a few other conjunctions are set off by a comma.

While strolling in the park, Loretta met a balloon man.

Though tempted to run away, the bear cub stood its ground.

Adverbial clauses are usually set off by a comma when they introduce a sentence.

When prices rise in the consumer market, the poor person feels the pinch first.

Although gold is said to be a precious metal, it is less useful than iron.

Here is a list of the most common subordinating conjunctions; when a clause begins with one of these words, you know that it cannot stand alone as a sentence. (Note that some of these words can also serve as prepositions; see Rule 8.)

after	even though	so . . . that
although	how	than
as	if	that
as . . . as	in order that	though
as if	inasmuch as	unless
as though	provided (that)	until, till
because	since	when, whenever
before	so (that)	where, wherever
even if	so . . . as	while

Some of the following sentences begin with phrases or clauses that need to be set off with commas; some do not. Rewrite the sentences that need commas, putting the commas in their proper places. If a sentence is correct, put a C in the space provided.

1. As Arnold started past the town bar, a drunk came flying out of the door and fell in front of him in the gutter.

    _____

    _____

2. On the front stairs, was a large black spider.

    _____

    _____

3. When Greg and Henry came out of prison, they promised themselves they'd never go back.

    _____

    _____

4. Just over the hill, there's a beautiful little lake.

    _____

    _____

5. If you do not come to school early enough, you have to park your car far out in the back parking lot by the science hall.

    _____

    _____

6. Before anything can even begin to be manufactured, it has to be carefully planned.

    _____

    _____

7. Because we are people, we need the feeling of belonging and of having our peers interested in our ideas.

_____

_____

8. Of the three sports, baseball is the only one with any great popularity.

_____

_____

9. Needless to say, they collided.

_____

_____

10. In order to demonstrate this, we will examine each step in the process.

_____

_____

Writing Practice

Write a paragraph about your experience with doctors or dentists. Include in it properly punctuated sentences using introductory elements of at least three kinds. Underline those elements.

_____

_____

_____

_____

_____

_____

_____

Use commas to set off the name of some-one spoken to directly, or to set off words of direct address used in place of a name:

Ellen, please fetch me my pipe.

Look sharp, **Mr. Ryerson**, or the ball will smash your glasses.

I'm warning you for the last time, **you little brats**.

Use commas to set off all items after the first in dates and addresses:

He died on July 13, 1848.

Our first address was 18½ Flager Place, Wilmington, Kansas 60712.

(Note that the ZIP code is not set off by a comma.)

The words set off by commas in direct address are usually names and may come in a number of places in a sentence.

Tom, please sit down when the bell rings.

Please, **Tom**, sit down when the bell rings.

Please sit down, **Tom**, when the bell rings.

Please sit down when the bell rings, **Tom**.

Sometimes elements other than names are used in direct address.

Gentlemen, welcome to Wilmette.

Girls, I have an interesting story to tell you.

Whoever you are, stop pounding on the door!

I say to you, **Rotarian brothers**, we face a crisis.

Remember to set off all items after the first in dates and addresses, with one exception: there is no comma between the name of the state and the ZIP code.

On Sunday, December 7, 1941, the Japanese attacked Pearl Harbor.

Deliver that package to 3944 Elm Avenue, Long Beach, California 90807.

Just as the ZIP code in the United States is not set off with commas, some elements of foreign addresses may not use commas either. If you have occasion to write to a foreign address, consult your Post Office. Here are two examples of elements in foreign addresses that are not set off with commas:

Holmes lived at 225B Baker Street, London **WC2**, England.

Eva's address is Brunnby Gard, Vreta Kloster **5901**, Sweden.

COMMA: Direct Address, Dates, Addresses

In the following sentences, there are some terms of direct address and some dates and addresses that are not set off by commas. Rewrite these sentences, putting commas in the correct places. If a sentence is correct, put a C in the space provided.

1. Be watching, class, for news stories on the coming election.

_____

_____

2. You should understand, Clyde, that this report is due tomorrow.

_____

_____

3. It was on May 12, 1977, that Louie went to see Muriel at 1145 Warwick, New Lenox, Illinois.

_____

_____

4. Mr. Jenkins was an excellent fencer.

_____ C _____

_____

5. My cousin is stationed at Fort Stewart, Haynesville, Georgia.

_____

_____

6. My boyfriend and I started going together on September 17, 1976.

_____

_____

7. Mom,I found a bunch of old toys in the basement.

_____

_____

8. When will you be in your office,Dr. Morgan?

_____

_____

9. Just write to the Ready Realty Company,1437 Waterside Street,Coastlands, California 93608.

_____

_____

10. The Declaration of Independence was signed July 4,1776, in Philadelphia, Pennsylvania.

_____

_____

Writing Practice

Give instructions to three friends (address them directly) on when and where each is to begin a treasure hunt. Use at least one date and at least two addresses in your instructions.

_____

_____

_____

_____

_____

_____

COMMA: Direct Address, Dates, Addresses

_____

_____

_____

_____

_____

_____

_____

_____

_____

_____

_____

Use commas to set off

1. "Yes," "no," and interjections:

   Yes, Pablo was something of a ladies' man.

2. Contrasted elements with "not":

   It was turnips, not carrots, that led to his good fortune.

3. Adjectives of equal value from each other:

   A long, cold, tiresome winter faces us.

4. "Jr.," "Sr.," and "Esq." after names, and degrees and titles from names:

   Paul Adams, Jr.

   Barbara Ward, Ph.D.

5. Use commas to provide clarity:

   The question is, is he really going to die?

Several uses of the comma do not relate to each other but are necessary so that sentences will read smoothly and clearly.

Commas are used to set off the words "yes" and "no," and interjections ("well," "oh," "ah," etc.—words that have no grammatical relationship to the rest of the sentence).

Well, I am pleased that you could make it.

No, Mr. Beatty will not be back in the office today.

Commas are used to set off elements in a sentence that are contrasted with the word "not."

He found he had to take courses he really wasn't interested in, not the ones directly a part of his major.

There were pears, not apples, in that pie.

Commas are used to set off coordinate adjectives from each other in a sentence. Coordinate adjectives are adjectives of equal value in a sentence, all of which modify the same noun or pronoun. Do *not* put a comma between the last coordinate adjective and the word these adjectives modify.

My friend's mother is a charming, gracious, lovely lady.

His farm was well-guarded by fierce, loyal, highly-trained dogs.

Commas are used to set off "Jr.," "Sr.," and "Esq." after names, and to set off degrees and titles from names.

He preferred to sign his name Howard L. Smith, Esq., rather than Howard L. Smith, Jr.

Carolyn Black, D.V.M., will be the featured speaker at the workshop next month.

Commas are used anywhere in a sentence where they are necessary to make the sentence clear.

Inside, the barrel was black. (As contrasted with something like "Inside the barrel was a squirrel.")

Later on, the road became so crowded that we were crawling along at twenty miles an hour.

The modern tendency is to dispense with commas unless there is a specific need for them. However, don't hesitate to use them in any case where they will increase the possibility that your reader will understand exactly what you have to say.

Some of the following sentences need additional commas. Rewrite these sentences, inserting commas wherever they are necessary. If a sentence is correct, put a C in the space provided.

1. Missy sang in the concert, not Merle.

_____

_____

2. The trouble is, is there something I can really believe in?

_____

_____

3. Yes, these horses wore fancy trimmings when they went to war.

_____

_____

4. A high, piercing whine came from the direction of the barn.

_____ C _____

_____

5. That's tuna, not salmon in the cat's dish.

_____

_____

6. Hey, come over here a minute, please.

_____

_____

7. No, I don't think Al has seen that article.

_____ *C* _____

_____

8. It was a bright, beautiful, joyous kind of day.

_____

_____

9. Within, the air was heavy and dark.

_____

_____

10. Outside, the house was dilapidated; inside, it was charming and neat.

_____

_____

Writing Practice

Write a paragraph on how to beat inflation. Use "yes" (or "no"), a person's name and title, and a contrasted element with the word "not" in your paragraph. Don't forget the commas!

_____

_____

_____

_____

_____

_____

_____

_____

Do not use a comma to separate

1. Subject and verb:

The man in the window▲ nodded know-ingly.

2. Verb and object:

The leading lady accepted with a deep bow▲ the applause of the audience.

3. Preposition and object of preposition:

He stole it from the ugly old man with▲ the yellow mustache.

4. A noun and an adjective immediately be-fore it:

It was a brilliant, daring, courageous▲ act on his part.

No single comma is used to separate a subject and verb in a clause, a verb and its object, or a preposition and its object. These items are closely associated, and a comma would incorrectly separate them. Of course, pairs of commas may be used with interrupting elements in any of these situations:

He **bought**, so they said, a **ranch** of 410 acres.

Most subjects, objects, and objects of prepositions are nouns or pronouns, but both noun clauses and gerunds may also serve in those functions. A noun clause has its own subject and predicate and acts as a noun in a sentence. It is a dependent clause, like adjective and adverbial clauses.

Whoever gets there first will get the tire. (noun clause as subject)

The winner will get **whatever is offered as a prize**. (noun clause as direct object)

They will give the tire to **whoever gets there first**. (noun clause as object of a preposition)

No comma separates the noun clause in any of these cases.
The gerund is the -ing form of the verb used as a noun.

Swimming is fun. (gerund as subject)

I like **swimming**. (gerund as direct object)

He is not dressed for **swimming**. (gerund as object of a preposition)

No commas separate the gerund in any of these cases, either.

Though commas may be used to separate adjectives in a series before the nouns they modify, no comma intervenes between the closest adjective and the noun.

The **meanest**, **stingiest**, **surliest** man in town lives on the corner.

Some of the following sentences have unnecessary commas in them. Re-write these sentences, eliminating the unnecessary commas. If a sentence is correct, put a C in the space provided.

1. During the last year he has had, more accidents than I've had.

    _____

    _____

2. It is a well-written, funny, book.

    _____

    _____

3. Marie fought hard and finally won, the game.

    _____

    _____

4. The cafeteria in the basement of, the science building has good food.

    _____

    _____

5. The banana is a yellow, brownish-colored fruit.

    _____

    _____

6. The two pictures, show how people earned their living in those days.

    _____

    _____

7. The stands, at which the goods are being sold, look rather shabby and dirty.

_____

_____

8. Once upon a time, so goes the fairy tale, an ugly toad, became a handsome prince.

_____ C _____

_____

9. They are going to keep offering larger, more powerful, cars each year.

_____

_____

10. The company, had an enlightened employee relations policy.

_____

_____

Writing Practice

In the following paragraph, eliminate any unnecessary commas by putting an "x" over each one that is unnecessary.

Cleaning a garage, is usually not much fun, but it can have its rewards. You can often find, a number of things, you thought you had lost, like an old fishing rod, or reel. Sometimes you can find things, that you don't even remember ever, having. In old boxes on back shelves, may lurk surprising, treasures of, considerable worth. I recently, discovered an old hula, hoop, a baseball glove, and a red, white, and blue, top, things I had long ago forgotten. However, I am definitely not, going to let my garage get crowded, and dirty again. I need the space, more than the treasures.

Do not use a comma to separate

1. The two parts of a compound subject:

The girl with the long dress▲ and her younger brother fished from the rocks.

Kings of smaller European countries▲ and presidents of small republics have almost no power.

2. The two parts of a compound predicate:

The girl with the long dress caught an ugly fish▲ and threw it back in the water.

Kings have no power▲ and exercise little influence.

Any clause may have a compound subject or a compound predicate or both. No single commas are used to separate the parts of compound subjects or compound predicates from each other (though, of course, a pair of commas may be used with interrupting elements in either case, like this: "The oldest
$\overset{\text{SUBJ}}{\text{boy}}$, who was mentally retarded, and the youngest $\overset{\text{SUBJ}}{\textbf{girl}}$ $\overset{\text{VERB}}{\textbf{lived}}$ first at home and then $\overset{\text{VERB}}{\textbf{moved}}$ in with an aunt.").

Two subordinate clauses related in the same way to a main clause may be coordinated. In such a case, no commas are needed between the clauses.

When the sun came out and the birds began to sing, I finally crawled into bed.

"When" subordinates both "the sun came out" and "the birds began to sing," so both clauses are subordinate, joined by "and" without a comma. The same sort of thing occurs with both adjective clauses and noun clauses.

Athelstan, **who raided France and whom all feared**, commanded only eighteen rather small boats.

He realized **that he was finally a success and that most of his troubles were now behind him.**

Use commas whenever they are called for, but never use them without good reason. Too many commas make choppy sentences.

Some of the following sentences have unnecessary commas between parts of a compound subject or parts of a compound predicate. Rewrite these sentences correctly, eliminating the unnecessary commas. If a sentence is correct, put a C in the space provided.

1. She cried, and laughed at the same time.

    _____

    _____

2. He thoroughly washed, and painstakingly waxed his car this afternoon.

    _____

    _____

3. Every man, and woman in the village despised the dictator.

    _____

    _____

4. They seem to take into consideration the problems that jobs, and money create for the student.

    _____

    _____

5. Wanda, who was twenty, and Tex, her brother, were both accomplished musicians.

    _____

    _____

Writing Practice

In the following paragraph, cross out any unnecessary commas.

Riding a bicycle, and walking are two alternatives to driving a car. Anyone who lives close to his or her work, and wants to save gasoline should try one

277

or the other. Besides saving gas, bicycling, and walking provide exercise and eliminate the annoyances of parking a car. Both older people living on a fixed income and younger ones just beginning their careers can afford to own bikes, and can use them for short trips even though they need cars for longer trips, and for carrying large packages. The best advice for anyone these days is buy a bike and ride it.

Use the semicolon to join two independent clauses when no conjunction is used:

> Butter is often expensive; how good it is depends upon the cow.

> Sports cars corner well; however, they are hard on tires.

Use the semicolon between items in a series when the items contain commas:

> He drove to Denton, Texas; Ponca City, Oklahoma; Winston, Alabama; and Miami, Florida.

In the discussion of fused and comma-spliced sentences (rules 2 and 3), the point was made that two independent clauses should not be run together without punctuation or with only a comma. When two independent clauses are closely associated, a semicolon (without a conjunction) may be used between the clauses.

> Everyone should aid the stricken people of the Third World; I, for one, mean to do my part.

When both independent clauses of a compound sentence contain many commas, the semicolon may replace the comma that ordinarily precedes the conjunction between the two clauses.

> At first, really in spite of himself, Professor Tower, the head of the English Department, put up with student grumbling; and yet, strange to imagine, he, this same Professor Tower, was named Grouch of the Year.

When each item in a series contains several commas, use a semicolon between items. In this case, semicolons take the place of the commas that would ordinarily be used between items in a series.

> The fellow was hard to keep track of, for he lived first at 79 Wilshire Place, Banning, California; then at 79 Wilshire Drive, Hollywood, California; and finally at 79 Wilshire Avenue, Hollywood, Florida.

> Do not just pop in a semicolon anywhere. It has specific and limited uses.

In some of the following sentences, commas are used incorrectly in places where semicolons should be. Rewrite these sentences, putting in semi-colons where they belong. If a sentence is already correctly punctuated, put a C in the space provided.

1. Although Mattie is really a very nice person, she does have a violent temper; fortunately, however, it only explodes occasionally.

   _____

   _____

2. The fellow had an enormous appetite: for breakfast he would have half a dozen eggs, a couple of slabs of ham, several slices of toast, fried potatoes, two or three bowls of oatmeal, and some kind of fruit washed down with cup after cup of coffee; for lunch he often had as many as six sandwiches, along with soup, chips, pickles, fruits, and half a pie; and for dinner he could consume two or three steaks, several potatoes, a couple of vegetables, salad, bread or rolls, and a double portion of dessert.

   _____

   _____

   _____

   _____

   _____

   _____

3. Seth, who was Jack's best friend, was a very intellectual fellow; Jack, on the other hand, was pretty much a playboy.

   _____

   _____

4. She hated school; therefore, she quit as soon as she was old enough.

   _____

   _____

281

5.   Danny is an unpleasant fellow; in fact, he's a real jackass.

_____

_____

6.   I don't want to go; furthermore, I don't want you to go, either.

_____

_____

7.   I'm sorry, but I have another engagement; otherwise, I would be happy to go with you.

_____

_____

8.   This can be answered simply; it is a place for learning, and that is its best feature.

_____

_____

9.   For Christmas she received a number of lovely gifts: record albums from her sister, her aunt, and her best friend; clothes from her mother, her father, and her grandmother, and perfume from her boyfriend and her godfather.

_____

_____

_____

_____

10.   I like to eat, so do many other people.

_____

_____

Writing Practice

Write a paragraph about a trip you would like to take. Include in it at least two pairs of independent clauses joined by semicolons and at least one series in which semicolons are necessary.

_____

_____

_____

_____

_____

_____

_____

_____

_____

_____

_____

_____

_____

_____

_____

_____

_____

_____

_____

_____

Use the colon to introduce a list or explanation:

He was cited for the following offenses: speeding, reckless driving, resisting arrest, and committing a public nuisance.

The foreman's reason for quitting was clear: he was afraid of the mob.

Use the colon between chapter and verse in books of the Bible, between the act and scene of a play, between the hour and minute in time designations.

Use a colon to introduce a list, an example, or an explanation. However, when introducing any of these elements, do not use a colon immediately after a verb or after "such as"; the part of the sentence that precedes the colon must be an independent clause—that is, it could stand alone as a complete sentence.

The parts needed were: a spoke, a pedal, a chain, a bearing, and two wing nuts. *(incorrect)*

The parts needed were the following: a spoke, a pedal, a chain, a bearing, and two wing nuts. *(correct)*

He got a variety of different things in the package, such as: cookies, a new scarf, two books, and his old harmonica. *(incorrect)*

He got a variety of different things in the package: cookies, a new scarf, two books, and his old harmonica. *(correct)*

In addition to its use in introducing lists or explanations, the colon is used to designate the chapter and verse in books of the Bible (Matthew I:14); to designate the act and scene of a play (Hamlet I:3); to separate hour and minute in figure time designations (8:14 p.m.); and usually to follow the salutation in a business letter (Dear Professor:).

Finally, the colon is used after headings in the text of books and magazines ("Introduction: The Causes of War").

In some of the following sentences a colon has been used incorrectly, or there are other marks of punctuation where a colon should be used. Rewrite the incorrect sentences correctly. If a sentence is correct, put a C in the space provided.

1. He gave an example of the principle that every action has an equal and opposite reaction; when you shoot a rifle it kicks back against your shoulder.

_____

_____

2. She came very quickly to a conclusion; he was incompetent.

_____

_____

3. Kenny gave the following reasons for his absence from school; high fever, low temperature, and a cold in his stomach.

_____

_____

4. My roommate asked me to buy the following items; a thick steak, some fresh asparagus, and two bottles of wine.

_____

_____

5. My solution to this great problem is as follows. We should appoint a student committee to try to raise the money to have this area paved.

_____

_____

6. I found one main difference: the onions were missing from the second salad.

_____

_____

287

7. That famous speech is from Shakespeare's play *Macbeth* II, 1.

_____

_____

8. I believe strongly in this principle: regardless of age, sex, ethnic group, or previous amount of education, everyone is entitled to as much education as he or she wants and can benefit from.

_____

_____

_____

9. I love rich, fattening foods, such as: cakes, pies, ice cream, and candy.

_____

_____

10. In order to fix the car, he needed: the new parts and the proper tools to work with.

_____

_____

Writing Practice

Write a paragraph on a favorite game or sport in which you include the colon used correctly at least four times in at least two different ways.

_____

_____

_____

_____

_____

_____

COLON

_____

_____

_____

_____

_____

_____

_____

_____

_____

_____

_____

To make possessives of either singular or plural nouns not ending in -s, add 's:

A man's home is his castle.

Children's stories always put me to sleep.

To make possessives of singular nouns ending in -s, add either ' or 's.

The ass's coat was rough and dirty.

Tom Jones' (or Jones's) daughter died young.

To make possessives of plural nouns ending in -s, add only '.

The dogs' coats were smooth and clean.

The asses' coats were rough and dirty.

Add 's at the end of singular and plural nouns not ending in -s to make them possessive.

Her mother's truck broke down on the dirt road.

Also add 's at the end of singular and plural compound nouns not ending in -s to make them possessive.

Her mother-in-law's car broke down on the freeway.

The sisters' mothers-in-law's birthdays were on the same day.

Add either ' or 's at the end of singular nouns ending in -s to make them possessive.

Boris' (or Boris's) teeth were yellow.

Add only ' at the end of plural nouns ending in -s to make them possessive.

The mushrooms' caps were gone.

Some indefinite pronouns can also become possessives by the addition of 's or '.

anybody's	no one's	everybody's	the other's
anyone's	one's	everyone's	others'
somebody's	either's	nobody's	
someone's	neither's		

In some of the following sentences, the possessive apostrophe is either left out or misplaced. Rewrite the incorrect sentences correctly. If a sentence is correct, put a C in the space provided.

1. The babies faces were fat and happy-looking.

    _____

    _____

2. My brother-in-laws' taste in clothes is atrocious.

    _____

    _____

3. What was the Beatles' influence on twentieth-century music?

    _____

    _____

4. The game will take place in the mens' gym.

    _____

    _____

5. The bus's brakes were faulty.

    _____

    _____

6. The stars positions in our galaxy are changing.

    _____

    _____

7. I think todays generation is trying to grow up too quickly.

    _____

    _____

8. Beauty is based on an individuals' preference.

    _____

    _____

9. To put myself in this ladys place would be a pleasant experience.

    _____

    _____

10. The tax collectors job is often a bad one.

    _____

    _____

Writing Practice

Write a description of how you would like to spend your ninety-ninth birthday. In your description, correctly use the following words in their possessive form: son-in-law, anyone, man, woman, child, celebration, friends.

_____

_____

_____

_____

_____

_____

_____

_____

_____

_____

_____

_____

_____

_____

_____

_____

_____

_____

Use an apostrophe to indicate exactly where letters have been left out in contractions:

I'm sure Jim'll be happy to have you.

Baby, it's cold outside!

Haven't we met before?

You can't or you won't?

Guess who's coming to dinner.

Many contractions come about with various helping verbs, such as "am," "are," "is," "will," "would," "have," and "had."

I'm	I am	he'll	he will
you're	you are	who'd have	who would have
it's	it is	we've	we have
they're	they are	they'd gone	they had gone

We use "not" to make negative forms of verbs, often with the helping verb "do." As a contraction, "not" becomes "n't" and is attached directly to the verb or helping verb.

I wouldn't know.	I would not know.
He doesn't know.	He does not know.
It isn't true.	It is not true.
They aren't ready.	They are not ready.

One helping verb changes form internally when it becomes a contraction.

He will not go.   He won't go.

Another one changes slightly by losing an extra letter.

You cannot go.   You can't go.

In any word with the contraction of "not," the apostrophe always comes in the middle: "n't."

There is a small group of pairs of words which often confuse people when they write because they are unsure of which one to choose. This confusion occurs because these words *sound* the same when said out loud but are really different words meaning different things. The important thing to remember is that if the word is a contraction, it will have an apostrophe in it. Here are the most commonly confused words:

Contractions	Possessive Pronouns
it's (means *it is*)	its
you're (means *you are*)	your
they're (means *they are*)	their
who's (means *who is*)	whose

There is an easy test to find out when you are writing whether or not you should be using one of these contractions. Any time you are confused, say in your mind the whole phrase and see if it makes sense. If it does, use the contraction; if it doesn't, the word you want is the personal pronoun. For instance, say "It is going to be hot tomorrow." "It is" makes sense, so you can use the contraction "it's." But if you say, "This is your book, isn't it?" it wouldn't make sense to say, "This is *you are* book, isn't it?" so you do *not* want to use the contraction "you're"; you want the personal pronoun "your."

Contractions are used more in the spoken than in the written language. Some teachers and editors consider contractions inappropriate for writing themes and other more or less formal prose.

APOSTROPHE: Contractions

In some of the following sentences, apostrophes are left out, or they are in the wrong place, or the wrong word has been used where a contraction should be. Rewrite the incorrect sentences correctly. If a sentence is correct, put a C in the space provided.

1. Your going on the field trip, aren't you?

    _____

    _____

2. We'll get our grades as soon as they're available.

    _____

    _____

3. I did'nt go to my cousin's wedding reception.

    _____

    _____

4. While shes doing all this, her son is on his own—free to do whatever he wants.

    _____

    _____

5. Theres nothing interesting or unusual about the writing in the advertisement.

    _____

    _____

6. It doesnt have a gas station on every corner.

    _____

    _____

7. She didnt look at me all night!

_____

_____

8. On Saturday and Sunday were always too busy catching up on the chores we fail to do during the week.

_____

_____

9. Its good to be a busy person, but we should balance it out with having fun.

_____

_____

10. He could'nt stand the thought of having a dirty-looking drunk lying in his gutter.

_____

_____

Writing Practice

Write one or two paragraphs briefly summarizing a movie you saw or a book you read recently. In your summary, correctly use at least six different contractions.

_____

_____

_____

_____

_____

_____

Use parentheses for incidental explanatory material not necessary to the meaning of the sentence.

The explanation is complicated (see page 9) but necessary to one's understanding of the rule.

Senator Thomas (Democrat, North Carolina) voted on every bill in the entire session.

Use parentheses around numbers in a list.

She brought (1) ice cream to her brother, (2) tarts to her father, and (3) eclairs to her mother.

Parentheses are used to enclose (would you believe it?) parenthetical material, that is, material which is only incidental or supplementary to the main idea of the sentence.

I tried (oh, how hard I tried) to convince him he was wrong.

Parentheses (parenthesis is the singular, but who uses one at a time?) are also used with figures in a list.

He had (1) mumps of a serious kind, (2) paresis, (3) advanced bronchitis, and (4) a chest cough; he didn't feel well.

Sentence and Writing Practices for Rule 31 are combined with those for Rule 32.

Use the dash for interrupting material or to show a sudden break in thought:

> Electric motors used to be—and sometimes still are—dangerous if not grounded.

> Ephraim Schwartz—you remember him from the Boy Scouts—inherited a pile of money from his uncle.

> I admit that I wanted—Charlie, look out!

Don't use the dash where some other punctuation mark is appropriate.

The main thing to remember about dashes is that you will seldom have any occasion to use them. If you are using them frequently, the chances are that you are incorrectly substituting dashes for more appropriate punctuation marks, such as commas or parentheses. Dashes are only used for interrupting or for showing a sudden break in thought. Dashes and parentheses are sometimes interchangeable.

> Jenny Shultz—she used to live on Pitti Pat Avenue—is now in the Peace Corps.

Or,

> Jenny Shultz (she used to live on Pitti Pat Avenue) is now in the Peace Corps.

When you are typing your papers, remember that on a typewriter, the dash is made with two hyphens without a space between them and the words they separate.

PARENTHESES, DASHES

In some of the following sentences, parentheses or dashes are used where some other punctuation mark would be more appropriate, or another punctuation mark is used where parentheses or dashes would be better. Rewrite the incorrect sentences correctly. If a sentence is correct, put a C in the space provided.

1. Perhaps—if there is time—we can get to the Grand Canyon on our trip.

2. I would like, but only if you think this is a good idea, to stop at my grandparents' farm for a few days on our way back from Chicago.

3. Why do you believe that—oh, there's a big spider in your hair!

4. I seem to have lost (not that it matters—they weren't any good anyway) all the notes for my term paper.

5. I thought I saw a—Joe, that boulder is falling right towards you!

6. Betsy Wells (my brother used to date her) is my roommate now.

7.   He might and indeed he should go on to college.

_____

_____

8.   If we can get Mr. Koch, how do you spell his name?, for sponsor, most of the
     class will be happy.

_____

_____

9.   The material for my term paper: see bibliography: came only from periodicals.

_____

_____

10. The best car I ever had (the first one) was a Chevy.

_____

_____

Writing Practice

Write a paragraph about your favorite season of the year in which you use
parentheses correctly in at least two different sentences, and dashes correctly in at least one sentence.

_____

_____

_____

_____

_____

_____

_____

Use a hyphen in compound words normally spelled with a hyphen and in compound adjectives:

> John's mother-in-law was a dyed-in-the-wool witch.

Use a hyphen to break a word (always between syllables) at the end of a line:

> He disappointed me, for he was simply incapable of telling the truth.

Use a hyphen to separate a prefix ending in a vowel from a word starting with the same vowel:

> I want to re-examine the latch.

Use a hyphen in two-word numbers from twenty-one to ninety-nine.

Hyphens are used within words, mostly to indicate compound words or to make words clearer. They are often as much a part of the word as the letters that make up the word and should be learned as part of the spelling: secretary-general, forty-seven, father-in-law.

The hyphen is used to break a word at the end of a line; but when you use it for this purpose, the hyphen *must* come between syllables: in-ter-est, man-u-fac-ture, hy-drau-lic, psy-chol-o-gy. The hyphen always comes at the end of the first line, not the beginning of the second, when you are breaking a word at the end of a line. If you don't know where the syllable breaks come in a certain word, consult a dictionary; do not just put a hyphen anywhere. Words of one syllable, no matter how long they are, must not be broken into parts at all: through, ground, breadth.

It is now common usage *not* to use a hyphen between a word and a prefix in front of that word when the last letter of the prefix is different from the first letter of the root word: rewrite, nonrestrictive. However, when the last letter of the prefix is the same as the first letter of the root word, the hyphen is still used for clarity: re-enter, pre-examination.

Two-word numbers from twenty-one to ninety-nine are always hyphenated when they are written out as words:

> He counted **ninety-four** wrens and **twenty-one** swallows on the field trip.

Numbers from one hundred up, however, are written as separate words, with no hyphen:

> There seemed to be **ten thousand** cars on the road.

> He had only **two hundred** dollars left for the month.

Some of the following sentences contain words that need hyphens in them. Rewrite these sentences, putting in the hyphens where they belong. If a sentence is correct, put a C in the space provided.

1. Reentry people, who have been out of school a long time, make up a significant number of community college students nowadays.

    _____

    _____

2. Mary's sister-in-law is a difficult person to get along with.

    _____

    _____

3. The philosophy professor assigned forty-five pages of reading for next Monday.

    _____

    _____

4. Tie-dyeing is a fascinating art.

    _____

    _____

5. When we were covering psychology, we learned how to handle day-to-day conflicts and serious problems.

    _____

    _____

Writing Practice

Write a paragraph on a topic of your choice, using the hyphen at least three times in at least two different ways.

_____

_____

_____

_____

_____

_____

_____

_____

_____

_____

_____

_____

_____

_____

_____

_____

_____

Use italics (underlining in handwriting or on a typewriter) for the titles of books, long poems, dramas, newspapers and magazines, art, the names of ships, and foreign words and phrases.

The name of Captain Ahab's ship in the novel *Moby Dick* is the *Pequod*.

Paradise Lost is a very long poem.

The Glass Menagerie is playing at the Shubert Theater.

The New York Times is the best newspaper in the country.

Newsweek is a magazine that does good objective reporting of the week's news.

Michelangelo's *David* is over ten feet high.

He showed a great amount of *savoir faire*.

Because typewriters do not have the special slanted type we call italics, we use continuous underlining to indicate in typewritten or handwritten work what would be in italics in print.

In addition to their use with books, long poems, dramas, works of art, the names of ships, and foreign words and phrases, italics are sometimes used instead of quotation marks to refer to words considered as words:

You have used the word *ambiguous* too often.

And and *but* are coordinating conjunctions.

Italics are also sometimes used to emphasize a particularly important or striking phrase; but there are usually better ways of achieving emphasis, so italics for this purpose should be used sparingly.

Some of the following sentences have words or phrases in them that need underlining (italicizing). Rewrite these sentences, underlining the words or phrases that should be underlined. If a sentence is correct, put a C in the space provided.

1. The New York Times decided to send its representatives to cover the convention.

_____

_____

2. Perhaps the most famous air ship of all time was the Hindenburg.

_____

_____

3. I really enjoy reading the magazine National Lampoon each month.

_____

_____

4. Many school children have to memorize lines from Longfellow's famous poem Hiawatha.

_____

_____

5. The most famous smile in the world is probably the one on the face of the woman in Leonardo da Vinci's painting, Mona Lisa.

_____

_____

6. *Esse est percipi* is a Latin phrase used by some philosophers that means "To be is to be perceived."

_____

_____

7. When the Titanic sank, hundreds of people lost their lives.

_____

_____

8. Most people know what hors d'oeuvres means, but not many people can pronounce it.

_____

_____

9. The play we're doing this season is The Diary of Anne Frank.

_____

_____

10. My sister's favorite book is Gone With the Wind.

_____

_____

Writing Practice

Write a brief report, on a topic of your choice, in which you use the names of two newspapers, one book, and two magazines.

_____

_____

_____

_____

_____

_____

_____

ITALICS

_____
_____
_____
_____
_____
_____
_____
_____
_____
_____

Use quotation marks for the titles of poems, short stories, articles, chapters in books, essays, and songs:

> Emerson's "Self-Reliance" is a strong statement on individuality.
>
> Poe wrote both "The Raven" and "The Tell-Tale Heart."

Use quotation marks to set off words discussed as words:

> He misused "irrelevant" six times in two sentences.
>
> A word often misspelled is "separate."

The titles of books, magazines, full-length plays, and movies are italicized (underlined on the typewriter or in handwriting); but the titles of shorter elements such as chapters in books, articles in magazines, poems, short stories, essays, and songs are set off in quotation marks. The practice is to use periods and commas with this sort of material in the same way they are used with directly quoted dialogue: they always go inside the quotation marks.

> Lorna read Christopher several passages from "Of This Time, Of That Place."
>
> After "The Lottery," any other story seems dull.

Quotation marks are *not* needed around the titles of your themes at the top of the first page.

Quotation marks are sometimes used to indicate words considered as words.

> You have used the word "ambiguous" too often.
>
> "And" and "but" are coordinating conjunctions.

For quotations within quotations, use single quote marks.

> Jinx asked, "Who here has read 'Gerontion'?"
>
> Eric replied, "I have read both 'Gerontion' and 'The Hollow Men.' "

In some of the following sentences, quotation marks are used incorrectly or
left out. Rewrite the incorrect sentences correctly. If the sentence is correct,
put a C in the space provided.

1.   The whole class enjoyed the discussion of Lamb's essay, A Dissertation upon
     Roast Pig.

     _____

     _____

2.   I thought that article on "how to buy a used car" was very helpful.

     _____

     _____

3.   I liked the story "Miss Brill" by Mansfield, but it's sad.

     _____

     _____

4.   The term freedom is often overused.

     _____

     _____

5.   There are often good articles in "Playboy."

     _____

     _____

6.   On the left side of the street a gang of men carrying clubs are attacking a truck
     with Fish written on the side.

     _____

     _____

7. The audience asked us to play God Bless America.

_____

_____

8. I recently read an article called "How to Get Into College."

_____

_____

9. On the penny are the words In God We Trust.

_____

_____

10. The Necklace, by Guy de Maupassant, is very moving when read aloud.

_____

_____

Writing Practice

Write a letter to a friend in which you recommend by title at least two of the following: a poem, a short story, an article, and an essay. Be sure to use quotation marks correctly around the titles, and be careful that any other punctuation marks next to your quotation marks are correctly placed.

_____

_____

_____

_____

_____

_____

_____

_____

_____

_____

_____

_____

_____

_____

_____

_____

_____

Use quotation marks around the exact words of a speaker:

> "Please bring in the clothes, Martha,"
> Mrs. Eldridge said coldly.
> "I won't do it!" replied Martha.
> "Why ever not?" Mrs. Eldridge asked,
> surprised by the response.
> "Because I don't feel like it," snapped
> Martha.

(Note that the comma is *inside* the quotation mark.)

In using the exact words of a speaker, use quotation marks around those words. When the same speaker's remarks run beyond one paragraph, each paragraph begins with quotation marks, but no quotation marks are used at the end of any paragraph except the last one of that particular speech.

"Tell us a story, Dad," begged little Ned.

"Well," said Dad, "you've been a good boy today, so I'll tell you the story of Helen of Troy. That's a favorite of your brother's.

"Once upon a time, in a land far over the ocean, lived a beautiful girl named Helen. She was the most beautiful girl in the whole Mediterranean world. She was Greek, very dark, with olive skin and deep brown eyes.

"All the boys wanted Helen for a wife. They kept pestering her father about her marrying one of them, but she had a mind of her own. That's what got her into trouble, as you'll see."

"Come, children," said Mother, "it's time for bed. Your father can finish tomorrow."

"Aw, nuts," said little Ned.

Sometimes people are confused about where other punctuation marks go in relation to the quotation marks when they are next to each other. Here are the rules (see Rule 18 for examples).

Commas and periods always go *inside* quotation marks.

Semicolons always go *outside* quotation marks.

Question marks and exclamation points go either inside or outside quotation marks, depending on whether they belong to the quoted material or whether they belong to the sentence as a whole.

Another confusing thing about the use of quotation marks is the matter of indirect quotations. Remember that you *never* use quotation marks with indirect quotations. Notice the difference between a direct quotation (the exact words someone said) and an indirect quotation (expressing the idea of what someone said, but not quoting the exact words) in the following examples.

Edith asked me the other day if you had gotten over your cold yet. *(indirect quotation)*

The mechanic said I needed a new left rear brake drum and new brake shoes on all four brakes. *(indirect quotation)*

The mechanic said, "You need a new left rear brake drum and new brake shoes on all four brakes." *(direct quotation)*

In some of the following sentences, necessary quotation marks have been left out. In others, they may be misplaced. Rewrite the incorrect sentences correctly. If a sentence is correct, put a C in the space provided.

1. You will probably look at the car again and say to yourself, "What does this guy take me for?

     _____

     _____

2. She said, "I am not going to get involved;" that's when I knew I might as well stop trying to persuade her to run for president.

     _____

     _____

3. "Where are you going"? Gretchen asked.

     _____

     _____

4. Mom told me to ask you "whether or not you and Julie are coming to dinner Sunday afternoon."

     _____

     _____

5. "Do you know where Dave is?" Jason asked.

     _____

     _____

6. Quotations from the past, like Patrick Henry's "Give me liberty or give me death"! are often useful as beginnings for speeches.

     _____

     _____

7. The carpenter said "it would cost me about $200" to have that cabinet built.

_____

_____

8. "Let's go," was all I heard him say.

_____

_____

9. The manager asked how old she was, and she said, I'm old enough to work here.

_____

_____

10. "Sergeant," he said, I hardly know where to begin.

_____

_____

Writing Practice

Write a dialogue (conversation) between two people about the high prices the bookstore charges for books. Have each person speak at least three times; have one speech in the conversation include at least two paragraphs.

_____

_____

_____

_____

_____

_____

_____

QUOTATION MARKS: Dialogue

Capitalization and punctuation of abbreviations vary. When in doubt about them, use a dictionary.

Abbreviations formed from the capitalized initial letters of names of organizations usually take no periods:

UN, AAA, IRS

Abbreviations of titles, addresses, and dates, as well as initials for names, require periods:

Ms., Jr., Dr., Ave., N.J., Aug., O. J. Simpson

Because both the capitalization and the punctuation of abbreviations vary so much, the only way to be sure about them is to look them up in a dictionary. Periods are the proper punctuation to use with any abbreviations that need punctuation at all.

Abbreviations made up of the capitalized initial letters of the names of organizations usually do not take periods.

The **UN** needs the support of all of us.

Nobody loves the **IRS**.

Abbreviations that may be used in sentences in themes include names of organizations, initials, titles, addresses, and abbreviations such as "mph" and "a.m."

Lt. Robert **A.** Jones, **USN**, **Dr. J. O.** Smith, **Jr.**, and **Ms.** Alma Stivers Johnson live at 42 Lexington **Ave.**, Holtan, **N.J.**

Otherwise, avoid abbreviations in sentences in formal writing such as essays, term papers, business letters, reports, etc.

She left a trail of cookie crumbs a **mi.** long. *(incorrect)*

She left a trail of cookie crumbs a mile long. *(correct)*

Where necessary, rewrite the following sentences, putting in the periods where they belong after abbreviations, or writing out abbreviated words which should not be abbreviated in sentences. If a sentence is correct, put a C in the space provided.

1.   There are 39.37 in., or 3.28 ft., in a meter.

_____

_____

2.   I usually get up around 5 am.

_____

_____

3.   She lives at 155 N Grove Ave, Portland, Ore.

_____

_____

4.   Some articles that have come out recently have accused the IRS of intimidation of private citizens.

_____

_____

5.   My 1937 Ford gets twelve mi. per gal. on the open road.

_____

_____

6.   The AAA is a useful organization to belong to.

_____

_____

7. He can get that car up to 150 mph!

    _____

    _____

8. John C Norton is my uncle.

    _____

    _____

9. Who is secretary-general of the UN?

    _____

    _____

10. Dr Jones moved to 213 North Ave, Sacramento, Ca in February, 1977.

    _____

    _____

Writing Practice

Write a letter to your local newspaper about some recent event. Properly use at least five abbreviations. (If in doubt, consult a dictionary.)

_____

_____

_____

_____

_____

_____

_____

_____

Use initial capital letters for the first word in sentences, for the pronoun "I," for some abbreviations, for all proper nouns, and for all proper adjectives:

> For years before I moved to Chicago, I lived in the East.
>
> The Christian tradition grows out of a Judaic background.

Most people begin each new sentence with a capital letter, and most people use a capital letter when they write the pronoun "I." Further discussion of these basic usages is unnecessary. Various kinds of abbreviations and their capitalization are dealt with in Rule 37.

Here are some other uses of initial capital letters.

• Use initial capital letters for the names of people: their first names, middle names or initials, and last names.

Esther is one of Mr. Williams' favorite employees.

I asked Agnes whether or not her middle name was Mabel.

• Use initial capital letters for the names of countries and continents.

The political philosophies of the United States and of China are very different from each other.

That summer I traveled through several countries in Europe: England, France, Switzerland, Italy, Belgium, Holland, and Germany.

• Use initial capital letters for the days of the week and the months of the year.

Sunday and Monday are my days off.

September and October are lovely months in this part of the country.

- Use initial capital letters for the names of cities and states.

I like to visit New York City to go to the theater and the museums, but it's too crowded as a place to live.

Maine and New Hampshire are particularly lovely places in the fall.

- Use initial capital letters for specific geographical features.

The River Styx is a river referred to in ancient mythology.

Mount Baldy is a favorite ski resort in California.

- Use initial capital letters for organizations and institutions.

The Ku Klux Klan is an organization that causes a lot of controversy in the United States.

San Antonio Hospital is considered a very good one in our area.

- Use initial capital letters to refer to religions and to the Deity.

Buddhism, Taoism, and Islam are three major religions of the world.

I have always believed in God, and nothing can shake my faith.

- Use initial capital letters for adjectives made from any capitalized noun.

European cars are often smaller than American cars.

Australian people speak a dialect of English that is quite different from that spoken by other English-speaking people.

- Use initial capital letters for titles used with proper names:

Chicago mourned the death of Mayor Daley.

My father does not share the political beliefs of Senator Watson.

- Use capital letters at the beginning of material in quotation marks when the material is a complete sentence.

The dentist said, "Open wider, please."

The instructor answered by saying, "Please feel free to see me during my office hours or after class."

340

• Use capital letters for the first word in each line of most poetry.

If this belief from heaven be sent,
If such be nature's holy plan,
Have I not reason to lament
What man has made of man?

• Use initial capital letters in the titles of plays, books, essays, films, chapters of books, and so on, for all words in the title except articles, conjunctions, and prepositions of one syllable. The first word of a title is always capitalized.

A Funny Thing Happened on the Way to the Forum

"I Have a Dream"

When words indicating family relationships are used as proper names, or are used as titles with proper names, they are capitalized; otherwise, they are not.

I asked Dad to take me to see his brother, Uncle Sylvester.

Gail's mother, sister, and aunt all went to Cincinnati to visit Grandmother Stone on her ninety-ninth birthday.

Some of the following sentences contain words that need to be capitalized but are not, or words that are capitalized but should not be. Rewrite the incorrect sentences correctly in the spaces provided. If a sentence is correct, put a C in the space provided.

1. I'd like to visit jackie next november.

    _____

    _____

2. Some of my friends are interested in the hindu religion; They believe in buddha rather than god.

    _____

    _____

3. Is Crater lake in California or Oregon?

    _____

    _____

4. We usually visit our Mother on New Year's Day and Christmas.

    _____

    _____

5. The company spokesman said, "let's all break for raisins."

    _____

    _____

6. The central intelligence agency has had many problems.

    _____

    _____

7. Is Maria french or spanish?

_____

_____

8. This city was formerly a village founded by the Indians.

_____

_____

9. On tuesday I have to go to the dentist.

_____

_____

10. This building is located on Fortieth Street, which is in manhattan.

_____

_____

Writing Practice

Compare two neighborhoods in your town or city. In your comparison, use
at least eight words that require initial capital letters.

_____

_____

_____

_____

_____

_____

_____

_____

CAPITALIZATION

_____
_____
_____
_____
_____
_____
_____
_____
_____
_____

CAPITALIZATION

Be sure to provide means for showing the relationship of one sentence to another:

Emmett kicked and gouged at my eyes whenever he could. **Nevertheless**, I liked him.

Or

In spite of the way he acted, I liked him.

Charlie Fox played every day for twenty seasons. He was called Iron Charlie. **Therefore**, he was highly respected both for his physical stamina and for his sense of responsibility to the team.

Individual sentences, even when they are clear and direct, cannot convey all that we want to say about a subject. Therefore we use sentences in conjunction with one another. When we do so, we must provide some way of indicating the relationships between our sentences. Otherwise our paragraphs will be jerky and unclear; the parts will not fit together smoothly.

We accomplish such integration of sentences in our paragraphs in several ways. The first of these is the inevitable relationship built into many pronouns; since they refer to antecedents previously stated, obviously they relate one sentence to an earlier one.

The second way is to repeat words and phrases. That is nearly inevitable anyway, and the repetition will tie the various sentences together.

A third way is to use the special words and phrases provided in our language for the purpose of showing relationships: in fact, therefore, otherwise, however, on the other hand, nevertheless, thus, and so on.

Notice in the following paragraph how the various sentences are related to one another by the three methods mentioned above. Those words that function in one of the three ways just discussed are italicized.

The topic of sports is *one* of the few subjects most high school and college students are willing to show real enthusiasm about. There are, of course, *those* few *who* are totally disinterested in *sports*; *however*, *they* are in the minority, since most *students* are interested in *sports* either as spectators or participants. In a way, *sports* seems a strange topic to be the one of almost universal *enthusiasm*, since *it* has little to do with the intellectual values *students* are supposed to be pursuing in *high school* or *college*. *In fact*, some people claim that *sports* tends to divert students' minds to an almost opposite *value*. *Nevertheless,* there is no denying that strong *enthusiasm* among students is usually expressed when the *subject* of *sports* is brought up; *therefore,* educators might as well work with that reality and attempt to interest *students* in intellectual values by utilizing the enthusiasm of *students* for *sports* as a way of developing rapport and getting ideas going.

Following are ten pairs of related sentences. In the space provided, make one sentence out of each pair, using appropriate transition words to make your new sentence smooth and coherent.

1. My best friend has traveled around the world five times. We call her "globe-trotter."

_____

_____

2. In school, math is the hardest subject for me. I like it.

_____

_____

3. The security guard threw us out of the building. We insulted him behind his back.

_____

_____

4. August was an unusually hot month. I liked it.

_____

_____

5. I don't know much about art. I love to visit art galleries.

_____

_____

6. Driving frightens me. I live so far away from work that I have to drive there.

_____

_____

7. Swimming is such fun. I go every chance I get.

_____

_____

8. Orange blossoms are tasty. I sometimes put them in cups of tea.

_____

_____

9. Dogs have a keen sense of smell. They notice many things we can't.

_____

_____

10. I am on the phone all day. In my job I have to call many different people.

_____

_____

Writing Practice

Write a paper of at least three paragraphs about a job you have or would like to have. Be sure to make it as coherent as you can. When you have finished, underline the transitional words you have used: the pronouns that refer to antecedents; the words and phrases you have repeated to connect them to ideas previously expressed; and special transitional words such as "therefore," "however," etc.

_____

_____

_____

_____

_____

_____

_____

TRANSITION

Use parallel grammatical structures for items in a sentence that are equal in importance and similar in function:

> He loves the mountains, the beach, and the desert. *(parallel words)*

> Sending flowers and writing love letters were his ways of wooing her. *(parallel phrases)*

> He swore that he would keep up with his homework and that he would get good grades this term. *(parallel clauses)*

Parallelism is used by writers for two reasons: to make a sentence smooth and coherent rather than jerky and awkward, and to give sentences rhythm, balance, and greater force. Notice how awkward a sentence may sound when nonparallel structures are used.

> He is slim, having blond hair, with blue eyes, and possesses graceful movement.

With the parallel elements put into parallel structure, the sentence sounds much smoother.

> He is slim, blond, blue-eyed, and graceful.

You should use the principle of parallelism in your writing whether you are dealing with words, phrases, or clauses. It is easy to make the error of using nonparallel elements when you are writing the first draft of a paper; so when you proofread, you should watch carefully for nonparallel constructions and change them to parallel constructions, so that your sentences will read smoothly and forcefully. Here are a few examples of typical nonparallel constructions and how they can be made parallel.

> A good mechanic must have thorough **training**, a mechancial **mind**, and **his hands must be dexterous.** *(nonparallel*—use of two words and one clause)

> A good mechanic must have thorough **training**, a mechanical **mind**, and dexterous **hands.** *(parallel*—use of three words)

Dr. McGill said that **eating a variety of types of foods** is much healthier than **when you eat mostly one type.** (*nonparallel*—use of a phrase and a clause)

Dr. McGill said that **eating a variety of types of foods** is much healthier than **eating only one type.** (*parallel*—use of two phrases)

Jarvis could not decide **whether to go on to graduate school** or **if he should start working** after completing college. (*nonparallel*–use of one phrase and one clause)

Jarvis could not decide **whether he should go on to graduate school** or **whether he should start working** after completing college. (*parallel*—use of two clauses)

Remember, when you write and when you proofread your papers, be sure that elements in your sentences that are equal in importance and similar in function are also grammatically parallel in their construction.

Some of the following sentences contain nonparallel constructions in places where parallel constructions would be smoother and more forceful. Rewrite these sentences correctly. If a sentence is correct, put a C in the space provided.

1. Sebastian wrote a term paper which was thorough, well-organized, interesting, and also showed a sense of humor.

_____

_____

2. She hopes that she can finish her apprenticeship in three more years and then to start her own business.

_____

_____

3. I intend to study all aspects of this issue carefully and therefore be able to analyze it rationally and come to a decision on an objective basis.

_____

_____

4. He worries too much about school, his girl, and what he will do after finishing college.

_____

_____

5. Cora couldn't decide whether to go to Europe with some of the other students during the summer or if she should take some more courses.

_____

_____

6. The panther is lithe, graceful, and moves incredibly fast when springing on his quarry.

   _____

   _____

7. Maury's jobs as a bus boy were to set the tables, filling the water glasses, and he had to clear the tables after the diners had left.

   _____

   _____

8. Abigail intended to study history and that she could learn German along with it.

   _____

   _____

9. I would rather get this whole thing over with right now than dragging it on into next month.

   _____

   _____

10. They both loved water-skiing, snow-skiing, and to take their dune buggy out on the desert.

    _____

    _____

Writing Practice

Write a paragraph of at least five sentences, on a topic of your own choice, in which you use at least one parallel construction in which the parallel items are single words, at least one in which they are phrases, and at least one in which they are clauses.

_____

_____

356

Spelling is a vexing problem in English because so many words do not follow consistent patterns. For instance, "though," "through," "enough," "cough," and "bough" should all rhyme, since they all end with "ough," but of course they don't. In various other ways, too, English spelling is chaotic.

Because the chances of spelling reform are slim at best and because many people consider spelling important, you are obliged to learn how to spell at least the words that you are likely to use in writing. (In speaking, you need to learn the way to pronounce words, not spell them—but that's another story.) Learning to spell isn't as hard as it sometimes seems, for almost everyone who writes English spells most of the words right most of the time. Even bad spellers misspell only a comparatively few words, and they usually misspell them the same way every time.

The best place to learn to spell is in school, because there you have someone to help you by pointing out your errors. (If you knew for sure which words you misspell, you could always look them up and produce flawless spelling.) You need to take advantage of this help by keeping a spelling list in which you record the words indicated to you as misspelled. That way you can eliminate one by one the errors that you have probably been making for some time.

Incidentally, you should never avoid using a word in writing just because you can't spell it. If it is the right word for your purpose, use it. Do the best you can with its spelling; look up the correct spelling in a dictionary, if possible, or ask someone how to spell it correctly. Then depend upon your instructor to detect any misspellings, so that you can learn the correct spelling systematically.

A couple of kinds of errors in spelling are rather special. The first of them has already been dealt with in the Handbook, under the use of the apostrophe. If you spell the plural of "boy" as "boy's," you have made a spelling error of one kind, but it isn't the same as if you had misspelled the root word. Careful study and application of the information in the appropriate sections of the Handbook should take care of this kind of spelling error.

The second kind involves the confusion of words which sound alike. It is not so much of a spelling error, for the chosen word may be spelled correctly, as it is an error of word choice. If you use "principal" when you mean "principle," you have committed an error of some kind, whether it be in spelling or in something else. The only way around the problem is to learn the difference in meaning between two words that sound alike or nearly alike but are spelled differently and then to choose the right one, correctly spelled, for the purpose at hand. Here are a few of the most commonly confused sets of words.

accept, except. To **accept** is to receive willingly: I *accept* the invitation. To **except** is to leave out: We will *except* him from the group requirement. **Except** is also a preposition: Everyone *except* the baby caught a cold.

affect, effect. To **affect** is to change or influence: His election will *affect* the conduct of foreign policy. To **effect** is to bring about: Her new attitude will *effect* a change in her children's behavior. **Effect** is also a noun that means "result": The *effect* of his activity was disastrous.

are, our. Are is a verb: All of us *are* wealthy. **Our** is a possessive pronoun: *Our* wealth makes us happy.

brake, break. A **brake** will stop a car or bicycle. If it doesn't, you **break** a leg. When you *brake* your car, you can avoid a *break* in the pavement.

capitol, capital. The **capitol,** a building, is located in the **capital,** a city. Also, it takes a lot of *capital* (money) to start a business.

complement, compliment. A **complement** completes: His tie *complements* his costume nicely. A **compliment** praises: I *complimented* him on his costume.

conscience, conscious. The **conscience** is the sense of right and wrong. To be **conscious** is to be mentally aware: I was *conscious* of her presence.

council, counsel. A **council** is a meeting or a group of people meeting together. To **counsel** is to advise: My advisor *counseled* me about my courses.

finally, finely. **Finally** means at long last or at the end: He *finally* arrived. **Finely** means in small pieces: Tom added *finely* chopped onion to the hamburger.

hear, here. We **hear** with the ear. **Here** is the opposite of *there.*

its, it's. Its is the possessive form of *it*: The dog bit *its* master. **It's** is the contraction for *it is*: *It's* cold out today.

passed, past. **Passed** is a verb form: The parade *passed* the stands late. **Past** is a noun or adjective: In the *past* she was a lawyer. Their *past* deeds betrayed them.

peace, piece. **Peace** is the opposite of war. **Piece** is a part of a whole: He ate a *piece* of pie.

principal, principle. A **principal** is the chief administrator of a school. A **principle** is a point in a code of behavior. The *principal* of her grade school taught her high *principles.*

stake, steak. A **stake** is driven into the ground. A **steak** is broiled and eaten.

than, then. **Than** is used in comparisons; **then** is an adverb of time: I arrived later *than* he did. *Then* Marcella showed up.

their, there, they're. **Their** is the possessive form of *they*; **there** is an adverb of place; **they're** is the contraction for *they are*: *They're* all putting *their* coats *there* in that closet. **There** is also used as a meaningless introductory word in such sentences as these: *There* is a fly in my soup. *There* are many flowers in Hart Park.

to, too, two. To means *toward*; **too** means *also* or indicates more of something than necessary; **two** is a number. She went *to* the store and on an impulse bought *two* fur coats, which was at least one *too* many.

weather, whether. Weather is wind, sun, rain, and so on. **Whether** is a conjunction introducing alternatives: He doesn't know *whether* to go or to stay.

who's, whose. Who's is the contraction for *who is*; **whose** is the possessive form of *who*: *Who's* going to tell me *whose* coat this is?

your, you're. Your is the possessive form of *you*; **you're** is the contraction for *you are*: *You're* going to regret *your* actions, my boy.

The first two sorts of spelling errors are relatively easy to deal with, then, if you are willing to take the time to do so. The third sort is a bit harder, for it involves the root spelling of the word. The spelling rules so often cited may be of little use in this matter, for they are concerned only with how to change the endings of words and not with how to spell the root words. (Most good dictionaries list those rules, and there are handbooks on learning to spell that also list them, so they are not included here.)

If you habitually misspell a word, it may be because you have not seen it properly. Since we learn to spell by eye, we must look carefully at a word to see the sequence of letters. Once we have the picture of the word in mind, future correct spellings are easy.

Here is a useful series of steps to follow in memorizing the spelling of a word.

1. Find out what the correct spelling of a word is. Don't guess about it; consult a dictionary, or your instructor, or a friend who is a good speller.

2. Look at the word to determine its general shape and the way the letters fit together into syllables and the whole word.

3. Write the word, looking at it carefully and saying it correctly at the same time. Check to be sure that you have copied it right; there's no use learning a misspelling.

4. Cover the word and write it from memory. Then check the spelling.

5. If you got it right, write the word from memory once more and check it. Then review it in the same way once a day until you are absolutely sure that the correct spelling of that word is an automatic part of your writing habit.

If you got it wrong, start again with step 2 and continue the series of steps until you learn the correct spelling by heart.

Long experience has revealed the words most likely to be misspelled by students. Here is a list of them. Maybe you can have someone give you a spelling test by pronouncing them for you to write down. Then you can apply the steps outlined above to the words you miss and begin to eliminate some of your spelling demons.

accept	attendance	controversy	environment
acceptable	attitude	convenience	equipped
acceptance	author	council	especially
accident		counsel	exaggerate
accommodate	basically	counselor	excellence
accompany	before	criticism	excellent
achieve	beginner	criticize	except
acquaint	beginning	crucial	exercise
acquaintance	believe	curious	exist
acquire	benefit	curriculum	existence
across	benefited		experience
actually	boundary	decreased	experiment
advice	business	decision	
advise	busy	definitely	fallacy
affect		denied	familiar
aggressive	capital	dependent	farther
all right	capitol	describe	fascinate
amateur	careful	description	favorite
among	carrying	desirable	fifty
amount	category	desire	finally
analysis	challenge	despair	financially
analyze	chief	difference	foreign
apparent	choose	disappoint	foreword
appearance	chose	disastrous	forty
appreciate	coming	disciple	forward
approach	comparative	discipline	fourth
approximate	completely	disease	friendliness
arguing	conceivable	divide	fulfill
argument	conscience	dominant	fundamental
arouse	conscientious	doubt	further
arrangement	conscious		
article	consider	effect	government
athlete	consistent	efficiency	grammar
athletic	consistency	efficient	guarantee
attack	continuous	embarrass	
attendant	control	entertain	height

362

hero
heroes
humorous

ignorance
imagine
immediate
immediately
incidentally
independence
intelligence
interest
interpret
its
it's

judgment

knowledge

laborer
later
leisure
length
license
literal
liveliest
lose
losing
luxury

maintenance
management
marriage
mathematics
meant
miscellaneous
moral
morale

naturally
necessary
ninety

occasion

occur
occurred
occurrence
operate
opinion
opportunity
optimism
origin

paid
parallel
particular
passed
past
peace
perceive
perform
permanent
personal
personnel
pertain
phase
philosophy
physical
piece
planned
playwright
pleasant
politician
possess
possible
practical
precede
prefer
prejudice
prepare
prevalent
primitive
principal
principle
privilege
probably
proceed
procedure
profession

prominent
prophecy
prophesy
psychology
pursue

quantity
quiet

realize
really
recommend
referring
relative
relieve
religion
repetition
represent
resistance
respectfully
respectively
response
rhythm
ridiculous

satisfy
scene
schedule
seize
sense
separate
sergeant
several
shining
significance
similar
sincerely
sophomore
source
speech
sponsor
strength
studying
subtle
succeed

success
succession
summary
suppose
suppress
surprise
suspense
symbol

technique
temperament
than
their
theory
there
therefore
they're
thorough
to
together
too
tragedy
transferred
tries
truly

undoubtedly
using
usually
unusual

vacuum
varies
various

weather
weird
whether
whole
who's
whose
writing

you're